CATHOLICISM IN FURNESS

Best Wishes to Jackie and Lucy

Anne C. Parkinson.

A History of Catholicism in the Furness Peninsula, 1127–1997

Anne C. Parkinson

Centre for North-West Regional Studies
University of Lancaster
1998

For 'Just My Bill' – who sowed the seed

A History of Catholicism in the Furness Peninsula, 1127–1997

This volume is the 37th in a series published by the Centre for North-West Regional Studies at the University of Lancaster.

Editorial Board: Elizabeth Roberts, David Shotter, Angus Winchester

Text copyright © Anne C. Parkinson, 1998

Published by the Centre for North-West Regional Studies, University of Lancaster

Designed and typeset by Carnegie Publishing Ltd,

Carnegie House, Chatsworth Road, Lancaster LA1 4SL

Printed and bound in the UK by Redwood Books, Wilts

British Library Cataloguing-in-Publication Data
A CIP catalogue record for this book is available from the British Library
ISBN 1-86220-055-6

Contents

Foreword

Anne Parkinson's history fills a much needed re-interpretation of Catholicism in the post-Reformation period. It will dispel considerable myth surrounding the strengths and weaknesses of the Catholic Church in this little-researched area of England, hemmed in, as it is, between mountains of the Lake District and the stunning shoreline of Morecambe Bay.

It is a tale of the rise and fall of a monastery, of grandeur and ruin, of birth, death and resurrection. It evokes the heroism and cowardice of the ordinary monks, priests, and people, of a region which owes to that monastery its patchwork of ploughed fields and its Trident submarine. It is an area of considerable natural beauty coupled with industrial wasteland: a microcosm of England.

I hope this scholarly, yet eminently readable book, will be widely used. Its Catholicity is far from being obtrusive and will advance the Cause of Christian Unity which involves 'speaking the truth in charity' (Eph. 4, 15)

The Right Reverend John Brewer
Bishop of Lancaster

Preface

The central concern of this book is to recount the post-Reformation history of Furness Catholicism, culminating in its renewed expansion in the nineteenth and twentieth centuries; but to set this in a wider context it is necessary to go back in time and cover Christianity from its first appearance in Furness, almost a millennium.

The medieval history of Christianity in the peninsula is generally well enough known, dominated as it was by the well-chronicled Cistercian Abbey. For that medieval account the reader is given a summary and is referred for further reading to the estimable works by Bouch and Jones, *A Short Economic and Social History of the Lake Counties* (1961); T. West, *Antiquities of Furness* (1774) and A. F. Beck, *Annales Furnesienses* (1884).

Lancashire Catholicism has been covered by the well-known recent works of J. A. Hilton, *Catholic Lancashire* (1994) and C. Haigh, *Reformation and Resistance in Tudor Lancashire* (1975), dealing primarily with that part of Lancashire south of Morecambe Bay; Lancashire North of the Sands including the Furness and Cartmel peninsulas – since 1974 parts of South Cumbria – have not been subjected to such research. It is my aim to fill this gap.

My interest is in the often-overlooked post Reformation annals of Catholicism in the area, in particular the seventeenth and eighteenth centuries. The impression given is that the Old Faith had completely died out. Research shows that this is far from the truth; it certainly reached its nadir during this period, but through an amazing series of events, the remnant survived, forming a spring-board for the revival in the nineteenth century.

I hope that these pages will prove of interest to more than my fellow Catholics. While I have put forward the facts of history as they affect Catholicism, it is not my intention to offer offence to any other tradition; those days of division are coming to a close and I hope that this book will rather be looked upon as an eirenical exercise. In the twelfth century John of Salisbury observed, 'through studying the chronicles of the past, men come to perceive the invisible workings of God'.

Acknowledgements

I owe a debt of gratitude to so many people who have assisted me in the writing of this book, that it difficult to know where to start. The first person must be the Right Reverend Brian Foley, retired Bishop of Lancaster who encouraged me and gave me the initial impetus to proceed. His kind assistance was of invaluable help; to the Right Reverend John Brewer, Bishop of Lancaster for permission to research in the diocesan archives, for his encouragement and for kindly agreeing to write the foreword for the book. To Fr T. G. Holt, S.J., and Fr Thomas M. McCoog, S.J., of the Archives Department of the Society of Jesus, Mount Street, London, both for their help and for permission to reproduce material from their archives.

My grateful thanks to Dr Michael Mullet of the History Department, Lancaster University for his reading drafts and for his advice on style and sources. My thanks to the staff of the Barrow-in-Furness Library who were assiduous in finding books for me from all over the country; the staff of the Reference Library, especially Mr Ron Smith without whose wide knowledge and help my task would undoubtedly have been much more tedious. The rest of the staff in the Reference Library also call for recognition, especially Andy Holgate who has born with me so patiently in my many requests for obscure volumes, and always with a smile. The staff of the Barrow-in-Furness Record Office, in particular Mr Aidan Jones. To parishioners of St Mary's who have passed on to me their recollections, and also photographs. To Mr Ron Turner, the Chairman of the *Churches Together in Barrow*, for information from the Minutes of that body, and also Mrs. Rosemary Hocking for details from the Minutes of the *Dalton Churches Together*. Acknowledgements also to *The North West Evening Mail* for permission to reproduce photographs; to Mr Sankey for permission to print some of his historic photographs; and to the County Borough of Barrow-in-Furness, for permission to reproduce the map from Fred Barnes book *Barrow and District*.

My thanks to Dr Angus Winchester of Lancaster University for his photographs. Apart from all these who helped me in the research, I owe a debt of thanks to my family, who have in so many ways been a source of encouragement, and practical help on the technical side of getting the text on disk and teaching me to become, at least partially, computer literate.

Grateful thanks are due to *The Kirkby Trust* for their grant towards the publication of this book. Also to the many people who have helped with their sponsorship; Bishop Brewer's generosity in particular and the contributions of Canon Francis Cookson, Fr Stephen Cross, St Mary's, Barrow-in-Furness branch of *The Catholic Women's League*, and the *North West Catholic History Society*.

Finally, my heartfelt thanks to the Centre for North-West Regional Studies, Lancaster University for accepting this book for publication.

Standard abbreviations in the endnotes

BM	British Museum, London
BRL	Barrow-in-Furness Reference Library
BRO	Cumbria Record Office, Barrow-in-Furness
CRS	Catholic Record Society
CW2	*Transactions of the Cumberland and Westmorland Antiquarian and Archaeological Society, New Series*
LRO	Lancashire Record Office, Preston
DNB	*Dictionary of National Biography*
L & P	*Letters and Papers, Foreign and Domestic of the Reign of Henry VIII, 1509–47*
PRO	Public Record Office, Kew
Sewell Letters	*College of St Aloysius Papers, Rixton to Wigan,* Archives of the Society of Jesus, Mount Street, London
SP	State Papers
Sp. Cal.	*Calendar of State Papers, Spanish 1485–1558*
VCH Lancs	*Victoria History of the Counties of England, Lancashire*

List of illustrations

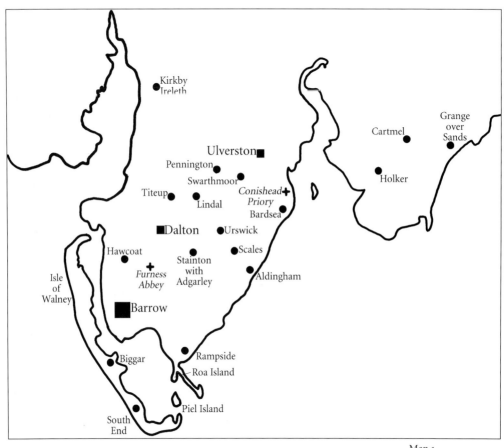

Map 1.
Furness and
Cartmel, with
principal places
mentioned in the
text.

CHAPTER ONE

Christianity in Medieval Furness

Furness Abbey

We have evidence from the archaeological discovery early in this century of fragments of two ancient crosses at Urswick Church, which were dated by the antiquarian W. G. Collingwood to the Viking era, that Christianity has been present in Furness from at least the ninth century. However, it was not until the twelfth century that there was an official record of the organised ecclesiastical history of the area. In 1124 Stephen, earl of Boulogne, afterwards (1135–54) king of England, gave to the abbot of Savigny, in Normandy, land at Tulketh, near Preston. Twelve monks under Ewain d'Avranches were despatched to England to take possession of their gift; subsequently, in July 1127 they left the banks of the Ribble for the remote, though well-provided, site in Furness, also granted by Stephen.[1] Communications with Furness have always been difficult, bounded as it is by the Cumbrian hills to the north and the Irish Sea to the south and west. The monks found in Furness all they could have wished for: a secluded wooded glen, solitude in plenty; and all the raw materials for building were at hand – sandstone, timber, iron, lead – and, most important of all, there was a freshwater stream. When the monks arrived the area was sparsely populated and only land at Dalton was cultivated, with small areas at Orgrave under the plough.[2]

Having established themselves at Furness, and built their abbey, the monks set about cultivating their extensive lands, and went about their prescribed tasks, singing the Divine Office and holding their daily chapter. For twenty-one years they continued under the rule of Savigny but in 1147 their order joined with that of Cîteaux. Richard of Bayeux, who had a high reputation for sanctity and learning, was chosen in 1148 by the Furness chapter as the first abbot following the filiation of Furness to Cîteaux and adoption of the austere Cistercian Rule.[3]

For nearly 200 years peace reigned in Furness, but in 1316, as recorded in the *Lanercost Chronicle*, Scots raiders marched south, 'laying waste everything as far as Furness and burnt that district ... taking away with them all the goods of the district with men and women prisoners ... and abundance of iron'. In 1322 a second invasion, led by Robert Bruce, occurred in even greater strength, leaving victims throughout Furness, Cartmel left in ruins and the economy of the district severely damaged.[4] These raids caused the abbey seriously to consider more adequate defences. A castle was built on the Isle of Fouldrey (Piel Castle) and at Dalton another was erected by the abbot out of the ruins of a still more ancient and extensive one.[5]

Following these Scottish raids, havoc was also caused by the Black Death,

FIGURE 1. Furness Abbey. (*Photograph: Angus Winchester*)

which ravished the country from 1348–50. The numbers of the monks had increased over the years but between 1379–81 a fresh visitation of the plague reduced their numbers considerably, for in the whole of Cumbria (Cumberland, Westmorland and Lancashire North of the Sands) the number of monks amounted to only 100.[6] Even so, the influence of Furness Abbey spread far from the comparatively small area of its first foundation; the monks acquired land in Cumberland, Westmorland and Yorkshire and founded daughter houses in the Isle of Man, Ireland and in Cumberland at Calder. Some of the endowments nearer home proved to be very valuable and broadened the activities of the monks from the purely agricultural to include the industrial. In 1384, Richard II granted a charter to the abbey of the mining rights of haematite ore at Elliscales and Dalton, along with those held by William Merton (or Marton) at Marton and Orgrave, all lying in the close vicinity of the abbey. This ore was smelted in High Furness where there was a plentiful supply of timber necessary for the manufacture of the charcoal used in this process.[7]

Recovery was evident: indeed, by 1500, at least in economic terms, Furness Abbey was at its zenith, though, unfortunately, evidence shows that its spiritual state had declined. The official visitor, Marmaduke Huby, Abbot of Fountains, acting as commissary of the abbot of Cîteaux, during his visitation of 1497 found Furness was faction-ridden. Two ambitious monks were contending for the position of abbot, but Huby, refusing to recognise either, persuaded the monks to elect Alexander Banke. The situation did not improve, for in less than three years, presumably after a period of deposition, Banke was rehabilitated by the chapter after absolution from 'incontinence' [unchastity], simony and other crimes. Fourteen years later the abbey was still in a state of faction, and the abbot of Stratford, another commissary, found it necessary to put in yet another abbot, who proved equally unsuccessful in bringing peace to this troubled monastery. During the resulting confusion a rival abbot found himself incarcerated in the London Fleet prison. As Dom David Knowles says, 'Furness . . . was probably past praying for.'[8] In spite of this sad state of affairs, all the information we have indicates that its tenants looked with affection on the paternalistic and hospitable Abbey of St Mary of Furness.

Religious instruction in medieval Furness[9]

The abbot of Furness held the most influential position in the whole of the Furness area and beyond, holding seigniorial rights over the peasantry; the abbey, dedicated to St Mary was also the spiritual power-house of the whole district. The people looked to the abbot for their material needs, and the majestic grandeur of the abbey was the embodiment of the spirituality of their faith. However, as important as the abbey was, it was not towards that imposing edifice that they looked for pastoral guidance but rather to their local parish churches and their incumbents. As Dalton was the capital of Furness, its church, also dedicated to St Mary, held pride of place, but the other churches in the area, such as those at Kikby Ireleth, Ulverston, Urswick, Aldingham and Pennington also provided pastoral provision for the commons, with a chantry chapel at Bolton-with-Adgarley which served as a chapel-of-ease from Urswick, and another at Bardsey (Bardsea). It was to these churches that the people would go for the celebration of Mass, to receive the Sacraments, and especially at death, it would be the priests from these churches that would provide 'shrift and housel' and their final resting place in the church-yard.

The Furness district was included in a vast, centuries-long Europe-wide missionary campaign to instruct lay people in Christian doctrine, adapting to their almost universal illiteracy through preaching, where this was available, notably through the work of the mendicant orders, especially the Dominicans and Franciscans, as well as that of canons regular, such as the Augustinian canons active at Cartmel and Conishead Priories.

Part of the task of such preachers was to insert approved Christian doctrine into popular mentalities largely occupied by folk beliefs, some of them perhaps of pre-Christian origin. Such a belief, which we today might label superstitious, lay in the ability of the priest, as a magus, to manipulate nature and control the weather. An ancient folk-story from Great Urswick,[10] recounting processions, confrontation between local laywomen and a priest, and the victory of the priest over the women through his mastery over the weather, water and nature, illustrates a long-standing belief in religion as a set of tools making for control over the environment.

A more developed – more 'spiritual' – Christian piety gradually arose throughout medieval Europe, centred on the Passion of Christ, the cult of Our Lady and devotion to the 'Real Presence' of Christ in the Eucharist. Vital to its developments were lay institutions, especially guilds and religious confraternities. Lay-directed organisations, the guilds, especially those centred on the Eucharist, played a vital part in raising the levels of lay religious education, notably through their didactic religious theatre. In point of fact, an understanding of the Eucharist, in literal and physical terms of transubstantiation, was highly developed amongst many lay people and was enshrined in the feast of Corpus Christi, established by Pope Urban IV in 1264, to honour and reaffirm the Real Presence, following controversies originated by Berengar of Tours, who suggested that the presence of Christ in the Eucharist was more symbolic than real.[11] The popularisation of the doctrine of the transubstantiated Real Presence gave rise to those guilds which, throughout medieval Europe, took the name of Corpus Christi. The ordinances of one of these, the Corpus Christi Guild at York, the city under whose episcopal oversight Furness lay, gave as its aim: 'the praise and honour of the most sacred Body of Our Lord Jesus Christ', and the principal object of its founders appears to have been to promote the decorous observance of the solemn festival of Corpus Christi. In 1426, the York city council issued an ordinance, 'that ... the solemn play of Corpus Christi should be played every year on the Wednesday, the vigil of the feast ...'.[12]

A good local example of the Eucharistic cult is a Corpus Christi Guild connected with Dalton Church in 1450, when Robert Harrington was parish priest;[13] at Kendal a didactic mystery play was performed either by a Corpus Christi Guild or by the Blessed Trinity Guild which we know was established in the town.[14] There is a well-documented story concerning an old man from Cartmel who was questioned in the early seventeenth century about his knowledge of redemption through Jesus Christ; he replied that he had certainly heard of a man so called because he had attended, in his youth, the Corpus Christi play at Kendal, where 'there was a man on a tree and the blood ran down'. The old man had seen the play as a boy and the dramatic effect had stayed with him to old age: a revealing insight into the impact these plays made on the people as they saw them year after year, first with children's eyes and then as adolescents and finally as adults.[15]

The only formal education available in medieval Furness was that provided by the monks at the Abbey. Indeed, the Abbey had two schools, a choir school for novices and a grammar school for the sons of tenants.[16] In 1582, forty-two years after the dissolution of Furness Abbey, its former tenants looked back with nostalgia to the days when this school existed.[17] By the early sixteenth century, its provisions were supplemented by the introduction of schooling at Dalton, where the vicar was the school-master,[18] and at Hawkshead, which at that time was within the parish of Dalton. Great Urswick had to wait until 1585 before a grammar school was established.[19] For those who had not attended the abbey school, their prayers would be learned by rote, their scripture from occasional plays and stained glass windows, and knowledge of the saints from the statues adorning their churches. The stained glass and the statues were employed to promote both religious teaching and to raise the levels of individual and congregational devotion: some fragments of the glass from Furness Abbey are to be found in Dalton and Windermere parish churches; however, the best evidence in our area of study of the use of stained glass as a visual aid to the didactic

FIGURE 2. Cartmel
Priory. (*Photograph:
Angus Winchester*)

preaching on the Sacraments, especially the Eucharist, can be seen in St Anthony's chapel, Cartmel Fell, where the east window depicts the seven Sacraments drawing their efficacy from the streams of Christ's saving blood flowing from the five wounds in the representation of the death of Christ on the Cross.[20] It is thought that this glass came originally from Cartmel Priory. Artistically accomplished and reflecting late medieval and especially Flemish iconographic styles, the window also incorporates advanced theological conceptualisation. We may choose to view it as an example of the teaching and preaching mission of the Augustinian Canons, with their foundation at Cartmel, and their deployment of the arts for doctrinal teaching to a high level. The original rood-screen of this chapel is also preserved, now split into three parts, hinged and forming the Cowmire Hall Chantry.[21] Renovation work in Great Urswick church earlier this century provided us with examples of murals, of empty niches showing evidence of images of saints and of the site of a rood-screen, all intended for religious instruction in visual form.

Marian piety and the development of an emotive devotion to Mary was particularly promoted by the Cistercian order.[22] Although no original statue of St Mary of Furness is known to have survived, a modern version was commissioned by the Old Girls of Our Lady's Convent School, Barrow, in 1938, modelled on the impression on the Great Seal of the Abbey; it captures well the centrality of Marian devotion in the Cistercian system. Devotion to Our Lady is also evident in the number of village churches in the area that took Mary the Virgin as their dedication. Urswick was no exception: its church was dedicated to the Blessed Virgin, and was commonly called St Mary-in-the Fields. Its additional dedication to St Michael may have been original through connections with Michael de Fleming who originally owned the land on which the church stands; alternatively, it could be the result of a cult of St Michael which spread rapidly along the shores of the Irish sea to Ireland, the Isle of Man, and the west coast of Cumberland, following the reported apparition of the archangel on Mont Saint Michel in Normandy in 710.[23] Apart from this evidence, which is tenuous, the additional dedication seems to have come into use at some point during this century, for earlier documents refer only to the choice of St Mary the Virgin.

FIGURE 3.
Urswick church:
pre-Norman
sculptured stone.

The Mass

Throughout medieval Christendom the Mass, with its limitless benefit of prayer for the living and the dead, took pride of place in the expression of corporate praise and faith. The medieval belief in Purgatory encouraged provision for souls through chantry chapels in churches, paying for the upkeep of priests to offer the sacrifice of the Mass for the repose of donors' souls and those of their relatives. Such chapels were to be found in the Furness area: at Ulverston, where a chantry priest was retained for this purpose;[24] at Bolton-with-Adgarley, lying between Stainton and Little Urswick, on land donated by the abbot of Furness in the early part of the reign of Henry III (1216–1272);[25] and at St John's at Bardsey (1404).[26] It was the intention of Henry Kirkby, of Kirkby Ireleth, that such a chantry should be built at Kirkby, and he made provision for it in his will of 1506–7, though, on his death in 1524, his brother Richard claimed that the land earmarked for the chantry belonged to his inheritance, thus provoking violence.[27] The resplendent Harrington Chantry at Cartmel Priory (1347) is another example of such provisions.

Hagioscopes, or squint holes are to be seen in many pre-Reformation churches; they were used either to enable lepers, who were segregated, to see the Host at the Elevation during Mass, or for those of the laity who would otherwise not have been sitting within a sight line to be able to view the elevated Body of Christ, or, as Dr Duffy believes, to give the chantry priest a view of the main altar so as to make sure that his enunciation of the Words of Consecration – and especially his Elevation of the Host –

FIGURE 4.
St Anthony's Chapel,
Cartmel Fell.
(*Photograph:
Michael Mullett*)

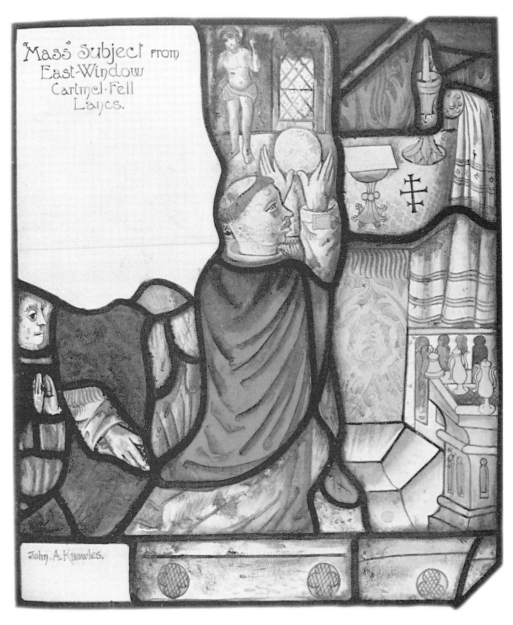

Mass Subject from East-Window Cartmel-Fell Lancs.

John. A. Knowles.

coincided with the main celebration. If this last explanation is the correct one, then the hagioscopes at both Aldingham and Urswick churches would indicate that there were chantries in both of these churches. On the other hand, and even without the requirement of simultaneous elevation in churches with chantries, we know that considerable efforts were made to give entire congregations a clear view of the raised Host, especially through adjustments, including hagioscopes, in churches where the layout of interiors built before the rise of popular Eucharistic piety impeded total vision. These adjustments would often necessitate the boring of holes in the rood-screen by the faithful, although there does not seem to be any evidence

FIGURE 5. 'The Eucharist' – detail from the Seven Sacrament Window in St Anthony's Chapel, Cartmel Fell.

of that in the Furness area. Sight of the Host, when the cry would go up from the congregations, 'Higher, Sir [the priest], hold it higher', was felt so important that a priest's stipend could be increased by private subscription if he extended the length of the Elevation. Alternatively, people would even be paid to support his arms so as to extend the duration of the Elevation.[28] Our Furness area then, was, clearly, no exception to the widespread medieval popular European belief in the Real Presence, whilst the district also provides evidence for the widely accepted deployment of the Host as a peace-making device. An incident at Kirkby Ireleth illustrates this. In 1524, a brawl occurred when Richard Kirkby took by force the court rolls concerning the chantry land his brother Henry had endowed in his will of 1506–7, but it was halted when the priest went into the church and brought out the Blessed Sacrament, standing between the contesting parties and holding the Host aloft for all to see. The fight ceased immediately, but the priest, who had been ready to start celebrating Mass, unvested and refused to continue until the men had been fully reconciled.[29]

Paradoxically, the increase of Eucharistic piety after the establishment of the feast of Corpus Christi does not seem to have resulted in an increase in reception of the Eucharist, though a devout minority communicated frequently. A feeling of unworthiness prevailed and the belief arose that it was 'the gaze that saved'. Substitutes such as the 'gazing' at the Host, as already mentioned, together with the distribution after Mass of 'holy bread' (ordinary leavened bread blessed by the priest before Mass), use of a 'pax', a representation of the Host, made of either wood or wax on which Eucharistic symbols were inscribed, came into common medieval practice: this pax,[30] was passed round the congregation to kiss, showing their peace with both Christ and with one another. The incident at Kirkby Ireleth where the Host was used as peacemaker was by no means unique, but was a common practice throughout Christendom, whether in Verona or Vienna, Florence or Furness. Evidence from Furness, both in documents and artifacts, convinces us, then, that the area, though, on the face of it, 'remote', was very much caught up in the currents of medieval European popular piety, including the cults of Mary, the Eucharist and the Saints. Attacks on the traditional rites were likely to provoke resistance, which was elicited in the 1530s by the Crown's campaign against the monasteries.

Notes

1. Thomas West S.J., *Antiquities of Furness, or an Account of The Royal Abbey of St Mary in the Vale of Nightshade, near Dalton in Furness, belonging to The Right Honourable Lord George Cavendish* (London: 1774, 2nd edn, ed. William Close, London: Walker, 1805), p. 66; For a modern account see F. Barnes, *Barrow and District* (Barrow-in-Furness: The Barrow Printing Co., 1968), pp. 1–37.

2. Ibid., p. 26.

3. West, *Antiquities of Furness*, p. 76.

4. Barnes, *Barrow and District*, p. 32.

5. J. Bulmer, *History and Directory of Furness and Cartmel* (Preston: Snape, n.d.), p. 79.

6. John Burgess, *Christians in Cumbria* (Kendal: Titus Wilson, 1982), p. 25.

7. Thomas Alcock Beck, *Annales Furnesienses: History and Antiquities of the Abbey of Furness* (London: Paynes & Foss, 1844), p. 11.

8. Dom David Knowles, *The Religious Orders in England*, 3 vols (Cambridge: Cambridge University Press, 1961), vol. 3, *The Tudor Age*, pp. 33–4.

9. For background of Christian instruction in medieval Europe, see, e.g., Bernard Hamilton, *Religion in the Medieval West* (London: Edward Arnold, 1986), ch. 7.

10. Bulmer *History and Directory*, p. 412.

11. For background to this controversy and the history of *Corpus Christi*, see Miri Rubin, *Corpus Christi. The Eucharist in Late Medieval Culture* (Cambridge: Cambridge University Press, 1994), esp. pp. 16–21, 164–81.

12. *The Register of the Guild of Corpus Christi in the City of York*, Surtees Society, vol. 57 (1872), pp. v–vii. The list of the Guild's members includes John Hawkyn, vicar of Aldingham (1411–12) (p. 13), Sir William Parr of Kendal, grandfather of Queen Catherine Parr; (p. 89, n.q.), Richard Ponsonby, abbot of Calder (1525) (p. 203, n.x.) the priors of Conishead and Cartmel (p. 203), and Alexander Rawlinson, abbot of Furness (p. 203, n.y.). Beck cannot date or place this abbot in his list: Beck, *Annales Furnesienses*, p. 116, but West Antiquities p. 124 gives Alexander Rawlinson as the abbot of Furness in 1510, preceding the penultimate abbot, Alexander Banke. See above n. 8 – This unidentifiable abbot could have been one not listed during the faction-ridden period of the late fifteenth and early sixteenth centuries.

13. *VCH Lancs*, vol. 8, p. 316, n. 120.

14. Charles M. L. Bouch and Gwilym P. Jones, *A Short Economic and Social History of the Lake Counties* (Manchester: Manchester University Press, 1961), p. 59; *CW2*, vol. 8, p. 131.

15. Charles Jackson (ed.), 'The Life of Master John Shaw', in *Yorkshire Diaries and Autobiographies in the Seventeenth and Eighteenth Centuries*, Surtees Society, vol. 65 (1877), pp. 138–9; The Cartmel story is cited in, inter alia, Christopher Haigh, *Reformation and Resistance in Tudor Lancashire* (Cambridge: Cambridge University Press, 1975), p. 68; *VCH Lancs*, vol. 8, p. 255.

16. Beck, *Annales Furnesienses*, p. 1.

17. Burgess, *Christians in Cumbria*, p. 28.

18. *L & P*, 12(1) 842.

19. Bulmer, *History and Directory*, p. 415.

20. J. T. Fowler, 'On The Painted Glass at St Anthony's Chapel, Cartmel Fell', *CW2*, vol. 12 (1912), pp. 297–311.

21. J. F. Curwen, 'St Anthony's Chapel, Cartmel Fell', ibid., p. 285. A rood-screen was a perforated wooden partition placed between the congregation's nave and the priests' chancel and was usually surmounted by a representation of the Crucifixion, with Mary and St John. Deemed 'idolatrous', they were usually destroyed at the time of the Reformation.

22. On the development of Marian devotion see Hilda Graeff, *Mary: A History of Doctrine and Devotion* (2 vols, London and New York: Sheed and Ward, 1963).

23. Henry L. Widdup, *Christianity in Cumbria* (Kendal: Titus Wilson, 1981), p. 28.

24. *VCH Lancs*, vol. 8, p. 346–7, n. 60a; C. W. Bardsley and L. R. Ayre (eds), *Registers of Ulverston Parish Church* (Ulverston, Lancs: James Atkinson, 1886), p. xxix.

25. Bulmer, *History and Directory*, p. 417.

26. *VCH Lancs*, vol. 8, p. 337, n. 172: Land was acquired in 1404 by the vicar Joannes from Hugh de Bardsey for which the vicar and his successors were to find a

chaplain to celebrate Mass, every Friday, at St John's Chapel in Bardsey, for the souls of Hugh and his family.

27. *VCH Lancs*, vol. 8, pp. 394–5, nn. 46, 47.

28. Johannes H. Emminghaus, *The Eucharist* (Collegeville, MN: Liturgical Press, 1988), pp. 80–1.

29. *VCH Lancs*, vol. 8, p. 395.

30. For use of the pax, see J. Bossy, *Christianity in the West: 1400–1800* (Oxford: Oxford University Press, paperback); also Eamon Duffy, *The Stripping of the Altars, Traditional Religion in England 1400–1580* (Cambridge: Cambridge University Press, 1993), pp. 114, 125–9.

CHAPTER TWO

The suppression of the religious houses

The first Dissolution

Against the background of the European Reformation[1] of the sixteenth century, from the mid-1520s onwards, King Henry VIII (1509–47) moved towards a severance both of his marriage to Katherine of Aragon and of England's ancient allegiance to the papacy. By 1534, Henry, married to his new wife Anne Boleyn, was declared Supreme Head of the Church in England and, with his reforming minister Thomas Cromwell determined to raid the wealth of the monasteries, commissioned a preliminary survey of monastic assets, the *Valor Ecclesiasticus* (1535). Following it, in 1536 by Act of Parliament all religious houses with an annual valuation of under £200 were deemed forfeit to the king.[2] The principle of dissolution was not revolutionary: for instance, within our area of study, in 1525, Cardinal Wolsey attempted without success to close Conishead Priory when he was founding his Oxford college and received papal permission to dissolve a further twenty-nine religious houses.[3] It was rather the scale on which this new suppression of the 1530s was planned and carried out that was unprecedented, and provoked resistance.

As part of a first phase of what was eventually to become a two-part and total suppression, under the 1536 Act of Dissolution requiring the suppression, and confiscation of the properties, of smaller priories of a value of under £200 per annum, both Cartmel and Conishead were to be closed; larger houses, including Furness, were spared for the time being. For those who wished to stay in religion, places were found for them in the larger monasteries, for those who wished to leave, capacities (pensions) were granted. The financial motive behind this phase of dissolution became evident when certain religious houses were offered the option of purchasing exemptions from closure. The prior of Conishead made an offer of 1,000 marks (£666) but, when pressed by the king's representatives to make a higher offer, refused, knowing that he could not afford to go above his initial tender.[4] By the time of the dissolution, the range of provisions made available by monastic houses of what was then Lancashire North of the Sands (of Morecambe Bay) had extended from a daily sequence of intercessory Masses for the souls of the faithful departed, through education with their two schools, hospitality for the poor and travellers, provision of care for the sick with their incredibly large infirmary with its own chapel, to guidance across the dangerous sands. On one small island in the Bay, still known as Chapel Island, a priest was in residence to celebrate Mass for these travellers. In addition, both Cartmel and Conishead kept bonfires lit and rang bells during storms to warn shipping.[5] Another important obligation of the Furness religious houses was the upkeep of the coastal defences of the area.[6]

The Pilgrimage of Grace

Having in mind, then, the extent of the range of secular and social, as well as spiritual and parochial, provisions rendered by the Furness religious houses, it should not surprise us that an acute sense of deprivation caused by the Dissolution of the Monasteries ignited active support in the district for the rising called 'The Pilgrimage of Grace' (1536–7), led by Robert Aske and taking as its banner 'The Five Wounds of Christ'. The major grievance raised by the Pilgrims was the suppression of the religious houses, which they sought to have re-instated; but their lists of complaint also show anger at all the changes in religion and society, including loss of material welfare, transport facilities, especially between Furness and Yorkshire, and educational provisions, since Henry's religious changes had been introduced.[7] The Furness area, though remote from London, was thought so sensitive that Cromwell considered it worthwhile to place a spy, an apostate friar named Robert Legate, in Furness Abbey, while hatred of the minister in Cumberland, Westmorland and Lancashire was reflected in popular satirical ballads directed against him.[8] In Furness and Cartmel, within a month of the outbreak of the rising, the armed commons around Conishead had restored the canons to their priory, soon followed by the restoration, at the request of the canons themselves, of the Augustinians to Cartmel.[9] These mass actions in Conishead and Cartmel should be understood in the context of the parochial needs supplied by these houses, for Cartmel served the village and district of Cartmel as parish church, together with the hill-chapel of St Anthony on Cartmel Fell; the canons of Conishead served the church at Pennington, celebrating Mass there, and were responsible for supplying a secular priest at Ulverston church.[10] Thus the people of Furness joined the Pilgrimage because of the suppression of Cartmel and Conishead but also because they feared for the survival of Furness Abbey and for their parish worship. At Cartmel further outrage was provoked by the confiscation of vestments and a chalice which parishioners claimed belonged to the parish and not the priory.[11] By 16th October, when the canons had been restored by the commons to Cartmel, they found them all (except the prior) most willing to return.[12]

Furness was thus solidly behind the rising, with the support of at least some of the monks from the abbey. With the connivance of the rest, sympathisers met the rebels, or 'pilgrims', at Swarthmoor near Ulverston to give them a massive donation of £20: they then marched with them to Dalton, where the prior called on the abbey's tenants, including those at Walney, to join the pilgrimage.[13] At Sawley Abbey, a small Cistercian house on the borders of Yorkshire and Lancashire, four monks intimated, when their house was dissolved, that they wished to stay in religion and were sent to the abbey at Furness. In fact, when the pilgrims reached Sawley they found all the community still living nearby, those sent to Furness having been returned by the abbot to Sawley, and very happy to reclaim their monastery with the help of the pilgrims.[14]

The Pilgrimage ended with a truce in October 1536; the rebels were given promises of the redress of their grievances; these were not honoured, causing further sporadic uprising in the following February which resulted in the indictment for treason of the rebels. Although the Pilgrimage eventually collapsed, local people had mounted a stalwart defence of the religious houses, though Cartmel was re-taken by royal forces and all the canons, except the prior, together with sixteen local men were indicted for treason at Lancaster; four canons and ten lay men paid with their lives.[15] Worship continued, rather pathetically in the now almost roofless priory; the lead, which was the first thing to be claimed as treasure for the Crown, had already been stripped. Conishead remained in the hands of its canons until after the rising failed but was then suppressed. The canons were indicted for treason but sufficient evidence could not be found, so they never came to trial.[16]

One of the complaints of the Pilgrimage's leader Robert Aske, had been the desecration of shrines and relics, a grievance close to the heart of Cartmel, one of whose treasures was a splinter of the True Cross which, after the rebellion, parishioners and inhabitants of the area petitioned to be allowed to keep and to continue with their devotions 'as heretofore'.[17]

After the commons were subjugated in 1537, the Crown's policy was to endeavour by every possible means to turn the people against the monks and in favour of change. Cromwell ordered all parochial clergy to preach in favour of the Royal Supremacy and disciplined those who refused: but the priests were reluctant to preach and the people did not want to hear them.[18] Cromwell now gained his intelligence by placing spies in the households of sympathetic gentry, who kept him informed of any criticism of the Royal Supremacy by the people and clergy in the whole of Furness. Thus the minister's highly efficient intelligence service, designed to pick up all expressions of complaint over government policy, had an outpost in Furness.[19]

The surrender of Furness Abbey

In common with all the remaining monasteries of England and Wales, Furness Abbey was in a precarious situation after the collapse of the Pilgrimage of Grace. Within its cloisters it had sheltered a monk, one Henry Sawley who had proclaimed that 'no secular knave should be head of the Church', a deliberately dismissive reference to Henry VIII for which he was indicted for treason. The vicar of Dalton had accused the abbot of not keeping the reforming Injunctions of 1536, and one of the monks, John Green, had rashly said 'the king should never make them an abbot but they would choose their own'.[20] This was presumably a reference to the practice of Cromwell, with the king's approval, of putting acquiescent monks in the position of abbots when a vacancy occurred.[21]

Treason at Furness Abbey was certainly suspected and investigated, and the earls of Sussex and Derby spread, with the connivance of the king, the rumour that the monks were lazy, disobedient and covetous. All the great northern abbeys were now under suspicion, for many had been active in support of the recent rising. Now, in the period down to 1540 all were seized by the Crown and individual abbots such as those of Jervaulx, Whalley and a former abbot of Fountains, William Thirsk, were convicted of treason and executed.[22] There was no doubt that many of the monks at Furness had indeed both expressed sympathy with the rising and had openly showed their support for it, but in spite of all the investigations, no evidence of treason against the abbot could be found: if there had been, there is no doubt that he would have suffered the same fate as other northern abbots, and the abbey would have fallen into the king's hands with no more ado. Even so, Furness was a wealthy and powerful abbey and it could not in the long term be allowed to stay in being.

Determined to secure Furness Abbey for the king, the Earl of Sussex summoned Roger Pele, Abbot of Furness, to Whalley Abbey on Easter Monday 1537.[23] the report of the hangings of the Cartmel men, and that of the Abbot of Whalley had reached him before he left. A tired, dispirited and depressed man, Pele was questioned by the king's commissioners, who could get nothing out of him. Eventually, after a long day, the Earl of Sussex 'assayed him to know if he would surrender his house' and found him 'of very facile and ready mind' to do so. The abbot returned with Sussex and Sir Anthony Fitzherbert to Furness on the 9th April where the monks were not of such 'facile minds' to surrender, although they were forced to capitulate; there in the chapter house, the prior and twenty-eight monks appended their signatures with that of the abbot. The deed of surrender was signed on 11 April 1537. Beck vividly describes the scene: 'The pen was passed from abbot to each monk successively and in a few minutes the lamp of St Mary's altar was extinguished for ever'.[24] It is part of the purpose of this book to show how wrong that statement is. The first of the great English religious houses to 'surrender', Furness set a precedent, incorporated in the Second Dissolution Act, 1539, retrospectively legalising the 'voluntary' surrender of the other abbeys which followed on that of Furness.

The monks were allowed to remain in the abbey until June 1537, when Robert Southwell, the receiver, arrived to supervise the stripping of the lead, receiving all the treasure and dismissing the monks. Southwell found the monks uncooperative, unwilling to be dismissed, and resenting the poor financial offer of twenty shillings apiece made to them. The Earl of Sussex, knowing how spurious the 'voluntary' surrender was, and having heard the complaints of the monks that their abbey had been 'fetched from them by politick compulsion', drew up a new 'surrender' for the monks to sign, which acknowledged that the original surrender was entirely voluntary. Great resentment was felt, and they were far from acquiescent when forced, under threat of harsher penalties, to sign the parchment in the Great Hall before five hundred of their neighbours, refusing to agree to the allegation made by the commissioners that the reason they did not intend to persevere in religion was their 'infirmity', or lack of zeal. They succeeded in getting their award increased to forty shillings, little enough, for the cost of their 'secular weeds' (lay dress) would eat up much of this amount; three monks who were sick and 'impotent' (incapable of work) were given sixty shillings each before being turned out to fend for themselves. The lay brothers and the servants numbering 140, were paid up to date, which amounted to six months arrears of wages, and turned adrift, in a time of great scarcity, to seek employment amongst the former tenants who came to take possession of the abbey farms. One hundred poor boys in the 'chapter school' (probably so called because it was held in the chapter house) were told to take a holiday and not return. The value of the smelted lead, and the valuables seized from the abbey amounted to £800. Abbot Pele was 'rewarded' with the rectory at Dalton where he had expressed a desire to reside.[25]

Locally, a mood of bitterness, division and violence accompanied the completion of the Dissolution of the Monasteries in the wake of the suppression of the Pilgrimage: thus, for example in 1538, one of Cromwell's spies, Sir James Layburn, reported to him that the minstrel Alexander Stotson, late of Cartmel, Lancashire, who was taken on 9th July, stated that Isaac Dikson of Windermere, 'smote him on the head with the pommel of a dagger and dashed a cup of ale in his face' for his refusal to sing the anti-Cromwell song 'Crummock' 'that he [Stotson] had sung at one Fayr-burn's house in Crosthwaite, Westmorland, in the time of the rebellion'. Dikson also wounded William Willan, the host of the tavern, in the thigh.[26] This was obviously a pub brawl which resulted in Dikson's coming to rest in the 'Toolbuthe', the gaol at Kendal. The introduction of religious change thus seems to have resulted in the violent polarisation of Furness society.

After the surrender, the abbey lands were retained by the Crown but eventually leased to John Preston of Preston Patrick and Under Levens until, in James I's reign, his son Thomas purchased the estate outright.[27] While the estate was under the Crown, permission had been requested, and given, from Henry VIII, in the latter years of his reign, for some stone to be used for the repair of Ulverston church, which had suffered great damage in a storm in 1540–1, when the spire collapsed.[28] The ruins of the abbey proved a ready source of dressed stone for any who wished to plunder it. Thomas took up residence in a manor house he had built on a site which incorporated what was still standing of the main gate-house;[29] he also made use of the readily available dressed stone. The Preston family continued to live in the manor house until the latter years of the seventeenth century. The house was eventually taken over and converted by the Furness Railway Company to become the Furness Abbey Hotel; then, after bomb damage during World War II, it was reduced in size to become the Abbey Tavern. This is now the last remnant of the historic house which became known as the Manor of Furness.

Notes

1. For a good modern study of the Reformation, see especially Euan Cameron, *The European Reformation* (Oxford: Clarendon, 1991).
2. For the background see J. J. Scarisbrick, *Henry VIII* (Cambridge: Cambridge University Press, 1968), pp. 439–40; Geoffrey Baskerville, *English Monks and*

the Suppression of the Monasteries (1937: paperback edn, London: Jonathon Cape, 1963), chs 5–7.

3. Roy Midmer, *English Medieval Monasteries, 1066–1540 (Summary of)* (London: Heinemann, 1979), p. 148.

4. PRO, DL 41/11/59 ff. 8–9.

5. PRO, DL 41/12/11, nos 12, 13. See also Christopher Haigh, *The Last Days of the Lancashire Monasteries and The Pilgrimage of Grace* (Manchester: Chetham Society, vol. 17, 1969), esp. ch. 6.

6. Carrolly Erikson, *Bloody Mary: The Life of Mary Tudor* (London: Robson Books, 1978), p. 183.

7. See Scott Harrison, *The Pilgrimage of Grace in the Lake Counties, 1536–37* (London: Royal Historical Soc. 1981), pp. 12, 21.

8. PRO, *L & P*, 11(1), 1086.

9. PRO, DL 29/158/26; *VCH Lancs.*, vol. 8, p. 341, n. 47.

10. C. L. Bardsley and L. R. Ayre (eds), *The Registers of Ulverston Parish Church* (Ulverston: James Atkinson, 1886), p. xxvii.

11. PRO, DL 41/12/11, nos 12, 13.

12. G. W. O. Woodward, *The Dissolution of the Monasteries* (London: Blandford Press, 1966), p. 96.

13. PRO, *L & P*, 12(1), 652, 841.

14. Christopher Haigh, *Reformation and Resistance*, p. 129.

15. PRO, DL 26/13/6.

16. PRO, *L & P*, 12(1) 849, nos 29, 1088.

17. PRO, DL 41/12/11 no. 21.

18. Haigh, *Reformation and Resistance*, p. 101; PRO, *L & P*, 12(1), 841, no. 3, 842.

19. For Cromwell's intelligence service, see G. R. Elton, *Policy and Police The Enforcement of the Reformation in the Age of Thomas Cromwell* (London: Cambridge University Press, 1966), passim.

20. BM, Cotton MS, Cleopatra E. IV, fo. 134; *L & P*, 12(1) 841.

21. Beck, *Annales*, p. 316.

22. Woodward, *The Dissolution of the Monasteries*, p. 100.

23. Barnes, *Barrow and District*, p. 50.

24. Beck, *Annales*, p. 349.

25. Ibid., pp. 352–57; Letter from Robert Southwell. Printed in full in Beck, in précis in *L & P*, 12(2) 205. For pensions paid to ex-monks, see Geoffrey Baskerville, *English Monks and the Suppression of the Monasteries* (London: Jonathon Cape, 1937), pp. 185–95.

26. PRO, *L & P*, 13(1) 1346.

27. CRS, *Lancashire Registers III North Part* p. 2.

28. *VCH Lancs*, vol. VIII, p. 343, n. 13; Bardsley and Ayre, *Ulverston Registers*, p. xxix.

29. West in his *Antiquities of Furness*, p. 207 suggested that the site of the Manor House (and therefore of the later Furness Abbey Hotel) was on the remains of the abbot's lodging. Modern archaeological study discounts this, and plans of the lay-out of the abbey testify to the gate house as originally occupying this site. The remains of the abbot's residence are reasonably well preserved, remains of a fireplace still evident, and stand to the north-west of the nave of the abbey.

CHAPTER THREE

The English Reformation

Henry and Edward

Following the Dissolution of the Monasteries, the suppression of the Pilgrimage of Grace and finally the surrender of Furness Abbey, our region was, by all accounts sullen and stunned, though, as we have seen also polarised. The authorities realised, after the surrender, that some immediate action was needed to establish stability among the commons of Furness who were living in fear of an insecure future. The pragmatic remedy applied was to allow the local people, ex-tenants of Furness Abbey, to buy the best of the farm stock.[1] During his reign Henry VIII vacillated in his Injunctions and religious changes, which, in general, were politically inspired.[2] There was a see-saw effect of acceleration and deceleration in religious policy which had an unsettling effect on the people. In the last seven years of his reign the king soft-pedalled, indeed reversed, religious change.

On the accession of Henry's son and heir, Edward VI (1547–1553), such reverses of change that Henry had made between 1540 and 1547 were abandoned; reform was re-introduced and indeed re-doubled, with a full programme of reformation involving devastating iconoclasm.[3] This programme once more brought home the effects of change to our region. The evidence for Edwardian iconoclasm in Furness can be seen with particular clarity in Urswick church of St Mary and St Michael. In the early part of this century plaster was removed from the chancel and nave, revealing fragmentary remains of coloured murals that had been, at some point during the Reformation, obliterated by whitewash. This renovation also revealed, on the chancel arch, two canopied niches, now empty, giving mute evidence to the destruction of the statues. The arch itself revealed indications of an original rood-screen, also a victim of the iconoclasts. High on the west front of the tower are three niches, two of which had their statues removed: the third still holds a very badly worn statue of the Blessed Virgin, a *Mater Dolorosa* that escaped destruction.[4] Such destruction came about as a direct result of the royal Injunctions of 1547. Following hard on their heels, the Chantries Act of 1547 abolished both the chantries and the guilds, and with them such customary pious provisions as the 'Morrow Mass', an early morning Mass for workers, and the 'Jesus Mass', a votive Mass much favoured by guild members.[5]

With the forfeiture of the guild and chantry property, there were rich pickings for the Crown and for those in the pay of the Lord Protector in the earlier part of Edward VI's reign, the Duke of Somerset. From a Catholic point of view, Edward VI's reign was a catastrophe. A wholesale attack had been launched on the old faith, and by 1553 the Reformation had been imposed by law.[6] In Furness, as yet, Protestantism was only a minority voice, though one that was beginning to be heard.

For some years there had been two priests in the Furness area with reformist leanings, both based at Dalton. William Rede, vicar and schoolmaster of Dalton, had preached against the pope's authority as early as 1533 and had been ordered by the archdeacon of Richmond's vicar-general, or commissary,[7] John Dakyn, to surrender to the abbot of Furness a book, *Unio Dissidentium*,[8] which contained Reformation theology, and which, in 1532, together with similar books, had been banned from importation into the country by a royal proclamation, on petition of the clergy in Convocation.[9] What is significant, though, is that the Furness laity did not take kindly to Rede's radical views: on one occasion, when Rede had been trying to preach against papal authority, his sermon notes were removed forcibly and he was man-handled by 'some commissary', probably John Dakyn.[10] In the same year John Henshaw of Dalton was also under suspicion of heresy, probably influenced by Rede, but he recanted and was put in the custody of the abbot of Furness until 1536, when he was ordained and took up his position as priest and schoolmaster at Hawkshead, within Dalton parish. Despite his earlier official recantation, Henshaw clearly still hankered after the 'new learning', for he was found to be preaching against the cult of the saints and images and inciting his school students to iconoclastic acts at Hawkshead. He was indicted at Lancaster in 1537 but, probably owing to the policies prevailing at Westminster, the charges were dropped and he was still at Hawkshead in 1539.[11]

The early Protestant activities of Rede and Henshaw notwithstanding, the dominant religious voice of Furness was that of tradition. Conservatism was, as we have seen, strongly fostered by the archdeacon of Richmond's commissary in Furness, John Dakyn, who encouraged the clergy to oppose, and do all in their power not to implement, the reforming edicts; in 1536 he urged the continued payment of the levy paid to the Holy See, Peter's Pence, and sheltered a Kirkby Ireleth priest reported to him for preaching against the Act of Supremacy; in a rural deanery synod held in 1536 in Dalton, commissary Dakyn led a condemnation of anti-papal legislation.[12]

The continuing strength of lay Catholic piety in our area can be further assessed from other evidence such as the 1544 will of John Cowper of Aldingham who bequeathed the substantial sum of 6s. 8d. for a candlestick to be placed in the high choir before the Blessed Sacrament. Similar traditionalism is evident at Ulverston, where, in 1542, Leonard Fell left 40s. to a priest at Ulverston, his namesake and thought to be his relative, to celebrate Masses for a year for the repose of his soul; in the will, in which he explained he would commit his soul 'into the hands of God … [and] the faithful company of saints'. Fell in addition bequeathed 'six pence to as many priests to pray for me on the day of my death, that may be gotten'. The local historian, the Rev. W. Bardsley, vicar of Ulverston, believed that the priests 'that may be gotten' might have been a reference to scattered and impoverished former canons from Conishead. It also seems likely that the priest to whom 40s. were left to celebrate Masses was the Leonard Fell named in the visitations of 1548 and 1554, and who refused to show conformity at the Elizabethan visitation of 1559.[13]

The entrenched conservatism of rural Furness, orchestrated by the archdeacon's commissary, John Dakyn, was also strongly reflected in urban Kendal, where, during the Pilgrimage of Grace, 300 parishioners threatened to drown their curate, Robert Appylgarthe, unless he acknowledged the pope, and not the king, to be the head of the Church.[14] The Kendal parish priest, Walter Browne, gave the congregation no such trouble, for he 'did bid the beads [recited the Rosary] in the church, and prayed for the bishop of Rome as Pope'; those few – about twenty-four – who objected to this received the same threat as the curate.[15] The strength of feeling at Kendal was expressed with force when the bailiff attempted, on New Year's Eve 1537, to read out in the parish church the 'pardon' of the Pilgrimage of Grace granted by the king at Doncaster; he barely escaped with his life: why should the commons require a pardon, which is granted for a crime? It was reported that 'They were sore aggrieved with him ... and said that he should die' unless they might be allowed to resume 'the old fashion' in religion.[16]

New Books of Common Prayer under Edward VI, in 1549 and 1552, signalled the march towards Protestantism in the realm. Other local symbols, though, – stones recently recovered from Urswick beck – provide mute yet eloquent testimony to bewildering religious changes in the England of the mid-sixteenth century: now incorporated into the base of Urswick church's baptismal font, the stones are believed in local tradition to have been part of an altar that was destroyed under Edward, restored, like her Catholic faith, under Mary and once more removed and desecrated when religious change was, under Elizabeth, yet again the order of the day.

Mary and Elizabeth

During Edward's reign, the number of ordained clergy nationally suffered a drastic fall, but what was even more significant was the reduction in the number of candidates coming forward for ordination, which fell to an all-time low, though they recovered in Catholic Mary's reign (1553–1558).[17] In 1547, in the new diocese of Chester (1541),[18] under whose oversight Furness now came, there were only six candidates offering themselves for the diaconate in Lancashire at a time when such embarkation on the route to the ministry meant acceptance of the sweeping religious reforms already in train. In sharp contrast, in 1555, only two years after Mary came to the throne, George Coates, bishop of Chester ordained a total of twelve priests, nineteen deacons, thirty sub-deacons and thirty-four acolytes. After Coates died in 1556, Cuthbert Scott[19] succeeded to the see of Chester and in 1557 his ordinations were even more numerous. In the following year, Bishop Scott carried out five ordination ceremonies, ordaining in total seventy priests, fifty-seven deacons, seventy-six sub-deacons and sixty-three acolytes: of the seventy-six sub-deacons ordained for the whole of the Chester diocese thirty-nine, more than half, were from Lancashire. Unfortunately, we do not possess specific numbers for Furness, but we may assume that these were in proportion. In that same year the first diocesan ordination ceremony outside Chester Cathedral took place in Preston Parish Church. Bishop Scott being unavailable, the Bishop of Sodor and Man, Thomas Stanley, himself a Lancastrian, performed the ceremony.[20]

The very high numbers preparing for the priesthood, or being ordained, in Lancashire were of young men who had had their upbringing in the unsettled period after Henry's break with Rome and their adolescence under Edward's reforming Injunctions, but who were undoubtedly eager to accept Catholic Orders under Mary. These young men were looking forward, so they thought, to a life of celebrating the Catholic liturgy. Instead, on Elizabeth's accession, many remained essentially Catholic priests, celebrating Mass for the recusant laity, accepting poverty and a hazardous life evading the law for the sake of principle.

Although Mary's reintroduction of Catholicism has been faulted for its lack of the dynamism of the contemporary Catholic renewal known as the Counter-Reformation, its essential conservatism, far from impeding its prospects in Lancashire, seems, on the evidence of priestly vocations, actually to have facilitated restoration.[21] Mary was cautious at first, wishing for unity in her realm, and in her first Proclamation in 1553, although she restored the Catholic religion and the Mass, she permitted the practice of the reformed liturgy, at least for a time;[22] there was no realistic prospect of a wholesale restoration of the abbeys to take in houses such as Furness. She told Renard, the Imperial ambassador, that she 'wished to force no one to go to Mass'.[23] She probably hoped that, with the return of Catholic practice and devotions, the new liturgy would gradually die out. Indeed, now that we realise that the introduction of Protestantism into England was far from being an inescapable, or even an entirely popular, process,[24] we can appreciate that the chances, given time, of a successful re-establishment of Catholicism, under the new archbishop of Canterbury, Reginald Pole, were remarkably promising, with the prospect that Mary, although not in the first flush of youth, should have a long life, and a marriage producing Catholic heirs. Unfortunately, Mary's marriage in 1554 to her cousin Philip II of Spain raised the fears of her xenophobic subjects – Catholics and Protestants alike – of a foreigner on the throne of England. The anti-Spanish reaction made the queen – a true Tudor – even more determined to reintroduce Catholic worship, and toleration gave way to repression. The fires in which almost three hundred Protestants, typically of the poorer classes were burned, between February 1555 and November 1558,[25] especially at Smithfield in London, are rightly notorious; they certainly did lasting harm to the Catholic cause, ensuring particular sympathy for the leading reformers Cranmer, Latimer and Ridley, burned at Oxford in 1555. In the event, Mary died childless and thwarted in November 1558, with a marriage that had failed to fulfil her expectations of either marital happiness, or of permanently making her faith once more that of her realm.

Elizabeth followed Mary on the throne in 1558: the following year saw the implementation of the Elizabethan Settlement of Religion, by which the Church of England was 'by law established', the Mass forbidden, the use of a revised Book of Common Prayer enforced, papal power abolished and the monarch declared 'Supreme Governor of the Church'. Although there were concessions to tradition in the liturgy and vestments of the Elizabethan Church, its essence was Protestant. With the enforcement of the Prayer Book came the obligation for church attendance on Sundays, refusal – known as recusancy – initially incurring a fine of one shilling – a good day's wage – later rising to twenty shillings per month: in 1581 a draconian law was passed imposing a £20 fine on persistent recusants. Some, in the face of these fines, became 'Church Papists', attending church but not taking the Sacrament, but for many the reformed liturgy, having lost the colour and ritual they were used to, failed to appeal to their senses, and they remained attached to the old faith.[26] Many parishes, hoping for the return of the old liturgy, held on to condemned liturgical items for many years. For example, as late as October, 1571, thirteen years after Elizabeth's accession, the church-wardens of Crosthwaite (near Keswick) in Cumberland still had chalices, thirty candlesticks, pyxes, censers, banners, a vast array of vestments and 'other monuments of popery, superstition and idolatry' of which they were ordered to dispose.[27]

Initially, Elizabeth's government left Catholics relatively untroubled: there were no executions in the early years of Elizabeth's reign, and indeed, during the period 1570 to 1603, the number of Catholic martyrs was fewer than two thirds of those Protestants who suffered in the brief five years of Mary's reign,[28] though a large proportion of those who did give their lives for their faith came from Lancashire. Indeed, it is possible that the earliest Catholic victim of religious change under Elizabeth was a Furness man, a native of Ulverston, John Christopherson, who was educated at Cambridge, and who became in 1542, a fellow of St John's College, and of Trinity College on its foundation in 1546. During Edward's reign Christopherson went abroad for religious reasons but was supported financially by Trinity College. Presumably, at some point he received Holy Orders, for when Mary ascended the throne he returned to England and was appointed Master of Trinity and nominated chaplain to Queen Mary. He was deputed by Cardinal Pole as bishop-elect of Chichester in 1556–7 and consecrated to that see 21 November 1557. On the second Sunday after Queen Elizabeth's accession, Christopherson preached at St Paul's Cross in London against Protestantism and was put in prison, where he died a month later.[29]

On the local level within Furness, opposition to change was typified in the rector of Aldingham, Robert Brooke, who managed to survive in his benefice through all the religious changes between 1546 and 1562. In 1559, he and two others from the parish, including his curate Robert Garner (or Gardner) were summoned to appear before royal commissioners. In 1562 Robert Brooke was called before the Privy Council to account for his resistance to the Settlement, and in 1563 resigned his living rather than conform to Elizabeth's changes. Another Furness priest who suffered deprivation of his benefice under Elizabeth was Thomas Dobson, vicar of Urswick, as also did Edward Pirrey from Dalton.[30]

The commissary of Richmond, under Elizabeth, Robert Hebblethwaite, John Dakyn's successor and, it would appear a kindred spirit, provided a lead to other traditionalists among the local clergy, including Brooke. Hebblethwaite was responsible, under the archdeacon, for the Furness Deanery, but in 1564 was himself called before the Church of England's investigative High Commission at York. The nature of the charge against him is not known, but in view of his later history it would appear that he was charged with maintaining Catholic teaching, practice and worship. He was dismissed from office in 1571 and became, as did Brooke and Dobson, an undercover priest, serving the recusant laity.[31] Furness, in fact, was well served by the ministry of priests deprived from other parts of Lancashire and doubtless seeking shelter in the peninsula's remoteness: James Dugdale, the deprived vicar of Garstang, is recorded 'serving' at Masses in Cartmel as late as 1590 together with Richard Call (or Cowell), the schoolmaster, both of whom 'used themselves as clerks at saying of masses'. William Battie, deprived vicar of Halton, also celebrated Masses in Furness in the 1590s. One Richard Bardsey, 'brother to one ould Bardsey of Furnis who was a great papist', was thought to be alive and living secretly in the area, although, in other sources, was reported dead. He was suspected of being a priest, trained in one of the new Continental seminaries, as was St John Boste; both being 'kepte very secretly in that countrie'.[32] [Furness] However, it was the priests who had resigned or been deprived, known slightingly as 'massing priests', who provided the lifeline that kept the Catholic faith alive in Furness until the seminary priests and the Jesuits came, from the 1570s onwards, to take up the reins.

The difficulties of the clergy were shared by the laity, many of whom became recusants, frequently aiding one another: for example Lord Paget's Catholic cook, Robert Warde, came to Cartmel in 1590 as a recusant seeking and receiving shelter, his master having fled abroad because of his Catholic religion: Cartmel was a village with a strong element of passionate resistance to the newly established religion, traceable to the dissolution of the Priory and the popularity of the Pilgrimage of Grace.

Neighbourhood solidarity was a binding force in early modern England and Furness was no exception,[33] for local Protestants tended to turn a blind eye to those of their neighbours who were still professing and practising the old religion, at least until or unless neighbourhood quarrels might result in disclosure: thus in Lindale in Cartmel, in around March 1590, William Beesley and Ellen Fiddler in a disagreement raised the issue of how many people were still hearing Mass. An inhabitant of Lindale, one Taylor, was reported as having a boat of his own in which, when any search was made for priests and recusants, he often conveyed fellow 'papists' and priests 'from Milne-throppe haven' into the 'hele of Man or Scotland'.[34]

Such movements were watched all the more closely in the light of the issue of national security highlighted in the late 1560s when the rival claims to the English throne of Elizabeth's Catholic cousin, Mary Queen of Scots, culminated in the Catholic-inspired Revolt of the Northern Earls of 1569, followed in 1570 by Pope Pius V's bull of deposition *Regnans in Excelsis*.[35] The old faith had become an issue of treason, compounded by a threat of Spanish invasion using such a natural point of entry as the haven at Piel Island, south of Dalton, for 'all that country being known to Dr Allen (who was born hard by the Pyle) and the inhabitants thereabouts all infected with his Roman Poison'.[36]

The prospect of invasion apart, 'Dr Allen' – William Allen, from Rossall in Lancashire – is better known to us for his foundation of a seminary, in 1568, at Douai, in the Low Countries, where many young Catholic Englishmen went to be trained as priests.[37] By 1576 the growing number of students at Douai had caused accommodation problems at the college and the foundation, on the site of an earlier pilgrimage hospice, of the Venerable English College at Rome, by Cardinal Allen – as he became in August 1587 – coped with the overflow.[38] The seminary priests from these two colleges landed in England from 1574 onward and in the next ten years over 300 came over. In total 471 seminary priests were active on the English mission during Elizabeth's reign of whom 116 were executed during this period; thirty-five actually fell into government hands while still in the ports of entry.[39] The priests who left these two colleges knew that there was a high possibility that they would be giving their lives for their faith. Those leaving the Venerable English College at Rome would make their vigil in what has come to be known as the Martyrs' Chapel there, on the night before they left for England. Jesuits, too, from houses established at St Omers, Louvain and Watten in the Low Countries, arrived from 1580. All these priests fell foul of the 'Treason Act', passed by Elizabeth's Parliament of 1571, which targeted all those who converted or reconverted to Catholicism or who were instrumental in a conversion, all those returning priests who had been educated abroad, and those who helped or harboured a priest, all these offences incurring the death penalty. In such circumstances of high peril the Furness harbour of Piel Island functioned as a point of swift escape in the latter years of Elizabeth's reign: it was reported that there was 'one little fleebott [dingy] kept by a gentleman or two in that country nere unto the Pilafurther which doth carry English seminary priests and papists ... and if the wynde serve they maie be conveyed in one hower by means of saide bott unto Scotland or the Isle of Man'.[40]

By the end of the reign of Elizabeth in 1603, Furness, which had established a key place in the survival of Lancashire Catholicism, had also become a focus of anxieties over the invasion. This chapter has shown that despite official pressure in favour of conformity, Furness remained heavily traditionalist in religion under the Tudors, aligning it to much of the rest of its county, Lancashire.

Notes

1. Barnes, *Barrow and District*, p. 52.
2. For the politics of the Henrician Reformation see Christopher Haigh, *The English Reformations* (Oxford: Oxford University Press, 1993), esp. pp. 121–36, 152–167; and Scarisbrick, Henry VIII, ch. 9.
3. For a full account of this iconoclasm see Eamon Duffy, *The Stripping of the Altars, Traditional Religion in England 1400–1580* (Cambridge: Cambridge University Press, 1993), ch. 13.

4. This statue was the focal point for the assembly of the procession recounted in the 'Urswick Tarn Legend': see above p. 3, n. 10.

5. Duffy, *Stripping of the Altars*, pp. 99, 370.

6. Socio-economic discontent caused by the debasement of the coinage and disputes over the agrarian economy added to the religious discontent: Haigh, *Reformation and Resistance*, p. 152.

7. The title of vicar-general and 'commissary' would seem to be interchangeable: we will use 'commissary' in the text for the office in question.

8. Hermannus Bodius, *Unio dissidentium, omnibus unitatis et pacis amatoribus utilissima ex praecipuis Ecclesiae Christiana doctoribus ... selecta, et iam denuo locupletata, etc.* (Cologne:1531. BL. 3908 DE 7.) This book was subsequently published at Antwerp in 1532 in French under the title *La première partie de Lunion de toute discorde*: (BL. 849 E4). Using various of the early Fathers of the Church, the author dealt with such subjects as: original sin, double pre-destination, faith and works, grace and merit.

9. PRO, *L & P*, 6, 287; Strype, *Ecclesiastical Memorials relating chiefly to Religion and the Reformation of it, and the Emergence of the Church of England under King Henry VIII, King Edward VI and Queen Mary I* (Oxford: The Clarendon Press, 1822), 1(1) 253–4; PRO, SP1/75 fo. 63.

10. PRO, *L & P*, 12(1), 842.

11. PRO, *L & P*, 6, 287; Haigh, *Reformation and Resistance*, p. 83.

12. PRO, *L & P*, 12(1), 842.

13. *VCH Lancs*, vol. 8, p. 324, n. 33; p. 346, n. 36; James Raine, *Wills and Inventories from the Registry of the Archdeaconry of Richmond*, Surtees Society (1853), vol. 26, pp, 49, 36; Bardsley and Ayre, *Ulverston Registers*, p. xxxi.

14. PRO, *L & P*, 12(1), 671(2).

15. PRO, *L & P*, 12(1), 384.

16. PRO, *L & P*, 12(1), 7.

17. Haigh, *Reformation and Resistance*, pp. 154–7.

18. The new diocese comprised Cheshire, Lancashire, and in 1537, all the former arch-deanery of Richmond, which included Copeland, Furness, Kendal, Lons-dale and the parts of Yorkshire adjoining Lonsdale with Richmond.

19. Cuthbert Scott, a Cambridge theologian, was sent to Oxford in 1556 to dispute with Cranmer, Latimer and Ridley. When the Uniformity Bill was passing through Parliament in 1559, Scott spoke against imposition of faith by statute. He was imprisoned in the Fleet on 13 May 1560, released at some point in 1562 or 1563, and confined to a radius of twenty miles from the town of Finchingfield in Essex. He escaped from there to Louvain where he died in October 1564: Kenneth W. T. Carleton, 'English Catholic Bishops in the Early Elizabethan Era', *Recusant History*, vol. 23, no. 1, May 1996, pp. 8, 12.

20. Haigh, *Reformation and Resistance*, p. 200: figures calculated from *Ordination Registers*.

21. For a summary of the European Counter-Reformation, see Michael Mullett, *The Counter-Reformation and the Catholic Reformation in Early Modern Europe* (London: Methuen, 1984).

22. Duffy, *Stripping of the Altars*, pp. 527–8.

23. Sp. Cal., vol. 11,131, cited in Carolly Erickson, *Bloody Mary: The Life of Mary Tudor* (London: Robson Books Ltd, 1978), p. 309.

24. See Duffy, *The Stripping of the Altars*, pp. 524–37; Haigh, *The English Reform-ations*, pp. 285–95.

25. David Loades, *The Reign of Mary Tudor: Politics, Government and* Religion *in England 1553–58*, 2nd edn (London and New York: Longman, 1991), p. 273.

26. For a good survey of the legislation, see G. R. Elton (ed.), *The Tudor Constit-ution: Documents and Commentary* (Cambridge: University Press, 1962). See also Patrick McGrath, *Papists and Puritans under Elizabeth I* (London: Bland-ford Press, 1967), pp. 53–5.

27. Bouch and Jones, *The Lake Counties, 1500–1830*, p. 60; *CW2*, vol. 45, p. 43.

28. J. D. Holmes and B. W. Bickers, *A Short History of the Catholic Church* (Tun-bridge Wells: Burns & Oates, 1983), p. 158.

29. *VCH Lancs*, vol. 8, p. 343, n. 7; J. Gillow, *Bibliographical Dictionary of English Catholics* (5 vols, London and New York 1885–1902), vol. 1, p. 485. *D.N.B.*, vol. 10, pp. 293–5.

30. *VCH Lancs*, vol. 8, pp. 326–7, n. 81, p. 346; Haigh, *Reformation and Resistance*, p. 119; App. 2, 'Resignations by possible conservatives 1559–1583', p. 335.

31. Haigh, *Reformation and Resistance*, p. 212.

32. CRS, vol. 5, *Unpublished Documents relating to the English Martyrs, 1584–1603* (1908), pp. 181–2; 221. St John Boste was born at Duffton, Westmorland 1543; on becoming a Catholic, he left Oxford University and joined the English College of Douai, was ordained priest and on his return to the English mission, after many narrow escapes was captured and examined September 1593 and hanged, drawn and quartered at Durham 1594: BM, Lansdowne MS 75, f. 44. *D.N.B.* vol. 5, p. 422.

33. Keith Wrightson, *English Society, 1580–1680* (London: Unwin Hyman 1982), p. 51.

34. CRS, vol. 5, *English Martyrs*, p. 182.

35. For further information on the Bull and Catholic reaction to it, see A. O. Meyer, *England and the Catholic Church under Queen Elizabeth* (London 1916; 2nd edn London: Routledge and Keegan Paul 1967), pp. 37ff., 76–90, 138–41.

36. BM, Lansdowne MS. 56, fo. 174. 'The Pyle' mentioned in this manuscript referred to the Pyle or Piel of Furness, the natural harbour and safest haven between the Mersey and the Clyde. It lies directly opposite to Rossall, Allan's birthplace, the Pyle lying at the northern and Rossall at the southern tip of Morecambe Bay.

37. Eamon Duffy, 'William Cardinal Allen 1532–1594', *The Venerabile*, vol. 30, no. 5, 1995, p. 15.

38. Ibid., p. 18.

39. Ibid., p. 20.

40. CRS, vol. 5, *English Martyrs*, p. 180. 'The Pilafurther' is synonymous with the Piel, or Pyle of Furness: see above note 36.

CHAPTER FOUR

Penal times – the Stuart period

The period surveyed in this chapter, 1603 to 1764, is crucial in the consolidation of a minority of defined Catholic recusancy in Furness, crystallising out of a more inchoate traditionalism. In the Stuart period in our region, as throughout England, the English Catholic community now took on social characteristics it would keep until the nineteenth century.

In 1603 the English Catholics, above all their 'seigneurial' leadership, hoped for much from James I, son of Mary Queen of Scots, hopes which James encouraged when, on his accession, he excused the recusants from the fines for non-attendance at their parish churches. It was expected that a relaxation of the Elizabethan penal laws would follow, and Catholic disappointment when they did not resulted in the disastrous 1605 Gunpowder Conspiracy[1] whose failure further alienated Catholics from James' government. Alongside the savage laws against priests, the Catholic laity faced swingeing fines for non-attendance at parish worship, or alternatively 'compounded' – paid a flat rate of two thirds of their estate to the Crown in lieu of the monthly fine. This drain on income or real estate enervated many landed gentry families which had previously remained faithful to the Catholic traditions.[2]

Although Furness was politically part of Lancashire, the fact that it was known as 'Lancashire North of the Sands' gives an indication of the geographic isolation from the rest of the Palatinate and the closeness of Cumberland and Westmorland which affected its history in general and the outcome of the Reformation in particular. As we saw in Chapter 3, central and north-west Lancashire was noted for its strong resistance to the Reformation, especially in the Amounderness area. On the face of it, rural Furness might have seemed likely to follow the example of those other districts of north Lancashire in which Catholicism remained strongly entrenched. However, the absence of sufficient Catholic gentry leadership was a key factor ensuring an eventual Protestant ascendancy in Furness, for, whether in those parts of Lancashire that retained the Catholic tradition, or in England at large, wherever resistance was maintained, it was usually owing to the proximity of a large Catholic household. In this respect, although Furness lay institutionally in Lancashire, socially, with only a few gentry houses rising above the level of peasant tenantry, it resembled contiguous and impoverished 'Cumbria' in its lack of a numerous patronal recusant gentry. Although, as we shall see, there were families of lesser gentry, such as the Bardseys and Knipes, both of whom sheltered Catholic worship in the seventeenth century, much of the responsibility for protecting the faith in the area rested, down to 1678 at least, on the twin pillars of the major families of the Kirkbys and the Prestons.[3]

A further consequence of the absence in Furness of a numerous powerful, affluent and closely affiliated Catholic gentry is that much of the onus for what resistance to the Reformation as existed in the sixteenth and seventeenth centuries came from 'plebeian Catholics'.[4] Such resistance was, however, facilitated by the shortcomings, at least initially, of official religious instruction. In particular, sermons, the main medium of official religious teaching, in a still largely pre-literate society, were seldom available; it was reported, for example, in 1578, that none had been preached since the Elizabethan settlement in Pennington, Kirkby Ireleth and Ulverston, and, as Haigh says, 'even when sermons were provided, they were not always appreciated':[5] we saw above[6] that as late as the latter part of James I's reign a Cartmel man admitted, or at least professed to admit, to total ignorance of salvation through Jesus Christ. Partly as a result of such shortcomings in official instruction, Catholic recusancy with a 'plebeian' or peasant base had become implanted during Elizabeth's reign. Whether or not it would survive Protestantisation would depend ultimately on the effectiveness of Catholic gentry leadership.

It was during this Elizabethan period that the Kirkby family provided such leadership: the resistance to the Reformation of the Kirkby family became evident in 1564, when the Bishop of Chester remarked that he 'knew of no justice then favourable to the Queen's proceedings in religion' and that Anthony Kirkby of Kirkby Ireleth, a 'good justice, was hostile', though John Preston of the Abbey, another justice 'was fit' [amenable].[7] Later, at presentments in 1623, Jane Kirkby, wife of Anthony Kirkby of Kirkby Ireleth, was reported as not having received the Sacrament in the Church of England, though hers was the only case reported in Kirkby Ireleth. At the same presentments William Kirkby of Kirkby Moorside, from another branch of the same family, was reported to have 'depraved [defamed] the minister by saying that he and all the ministers in Lancashire preached more for their wages than their conscience'.[8] Jane Kirkby's husband was not reported at this visitation, though the family were recorded as recusants,[9] raising the possibility that the couple had both become 'Church Papists', thereby conforming to a pattern of family life that was common amongst the English Catholics: the husband would conform to retain the family's estates intact, but the wife and mother, who had the responsibility for the children's upbringing would refuse and keep the faith. The Kirkby family did indeed remain privately faithful to the old faith, having their own private chapel, until, as with so many other Catholic families, they capitulated at the time of the Titus Oates plot in 1678.[10]

Meanwhile, though, the Prestons of Furness emerged as foremost protectors of Catholicism within the district, on what we might describe as the 'Lancashire model' of gentry patronage. From evidence just cited that John Preston was considered 'fit' as a justice in 1564, it is reasonable to assume that the Preston family had conformed to Protestantism, prior to receiving the abbey lands, but Thomas, the grandson of the first John Preston, who died at the Manor in 1604, married a Catholic, a daughter of John Westby, a notable Catholic, of Mowbreck Hall, Lancashire, and his son John appears on the Recusant Rolls from 1593 till his death in 1643.[11] In the 1630–1 Rolls

John Preston is included as having compounded for two-thirds of his estate at £80.[12] The Prestons of the Furness Manor persisted in their adherence to the Catholic faith during the whole of their tenancy, providing patronal support to the local recusants and the opportunity for Catholic worship. The Prestons of Holker likewise remained steadfast until 1678, when they conformed and gained possession of the Manor estates.

Under such gentry tutelage, non-gentry recusancy survived in Furness between the late sixteenth and the earlier seventeenth centuries, down to the outbreak of the Civil War in 1642. Among the non-gentry recusants there is evidence for the women's occupying the role of 'defenders of the faith'. The examples cited above, of Jane Kirkby and of Thomas Preston's Catholic wife, the mother of John the recorded recusant, are prime cases of women's domestic and familial leadership of the faith and community. A further instance of female Catholic leadership coming from within our region arises from the Recusant Rolls for 1593–4 which record a fine of £100, an enormous sum by modern valuation – probably in arrears of fines – on Mary Singleton, spinster [occupation not marital status], wife of Thomas Singleton, previously of Scales (Newton-with Scales), and Elizabeth Calvert, alias Browne, also formerly of Newton-with-Scales, spinster.[13] In the following year Mary Singleton was fined £40.[14] The Rolls of 1630–1 record the compounding of fines by Bridget Bushel of Ulverston for two-thirds of her estate at £10 in lieu.[15] These women were only a few of what must have been a much larger body of recusants, for at the visitation at Kirkby Ireleth in 1623, although only Jane Kirkby was reported, the inhabitants were said to practise 'popish customs', even though it was admitted that there was no 'pernicious superstitious intent' – probably meaning that their actions were deemed to derive from traditional folk customs rather than from conscious Catholicism. The pre-eminence of women in the overall picture of Furness recusancy during this period is consistent with the fact that in 1641, of the total Catholic recusant population of Lancashire, sixty-two per cent were women.[16]

Within our area, the strongest evidence of plebeian recusancy comes from Dalton: when the plague came to that town in 1631, the population stood at 612 inhabitants, but after the plague had raged for seven months, fifty per cent of the population of both Dalton and Walney had died. Yet in spite of such heavy population losses, in 1641, five unnamed gentlemen and forty-two commoners of Dalton were presented as convicted recusants at the Lancashire Quarter Sessions.[17] These figures indicate that, whatever the prospects of Furness gentry Catholic leadership, which were, on the whole, unreliable, the area of south Furness is remarkable in the period down to the Civil War in harbouring a sizeable quota of peasant recusants: forty-two commons, fifteen per cent of the population in Dalton. To appreciate the significance of this figure one must look at the rest of England: in 1641–2, the recusant population of the thirteen counties showing the highest proportion of Catholics show an average of 2.7 per cent. of the population as a whole. Even though, as we have shown, Furness can not be equated with the rest of Lancashire, especially the Amounderness area, in the overall strength of its recusancy, yet in this small pocket of resistance within Furness we have the amazingly high figure of fifteen per cent, while the recusant proportion for the whole of Lancashire is only nine per cent.[18] The conclusion we can draw from these figures is that Furness or, at least, the area in and around Dalton, represents one of the stray pockets of resistance of Lancashire as a whole. In the longer term, however, it would have been difficult to sustain this lower-class recusancy without powerful and durable gentry protection.

This strikingly high recusancy rate in Dalton leads us to ask 'why'? We might speculate that one possible reason could be the fact that Dalton was the only township of any size in Furness. With the exception of the then smaller market town of Ulverston, the dwellings in the rest of both High and Low Furness consisted of villages or hamlets whose inhabitants were thinly spread over a large area where it would be easy to detect the odd Catholic who failed to attend the local church. Dalton, the ancient capital of Furness, on the other hand was a town with a market charter dating from Edward the Confessor (1042–1066), and with a thriving domestic economy. The sense of community in this small but busy town might well mean that each Catholic recusant would draw support from another under the umbrella of patronage given by the five lesser gentry surrounding the town. The possibility of a lingering 'folk memory' of allegiance to the abbey and the polarisation of the Pilgrimage of Grace should also be taken into account.

From the late sixteenth century onward, earlier shortfalls in Protestant missionary efforts, were being made good, notably by the special Lancashire scheme (applying, of course, to Furness), of the King's/Queen's Preachers; individual pastors such as Aldingham's rector from 1577, Richard Gilpin, brother of Bernard, the Protestant 'apostle of the north', helped spearhead the more intensive introduction of Protestantism into the peninsula.[19] By the time of the outbreak of the Civil War in 1642, Protestantism had made undoubted headway in Furness.

The preservation of Catholicism in our area was to depend ultimately on the roles, attitudes and persistence in their religion of a group of recusant families, the Prestons, Kirkbys, Bardseys, Knipes and Rawlinsons, on whom much of the interest in the remainder of this chapter must, inevitably, focus. We shall see that the capacity of such families to sustain 'plebeian recusancy' in Furness was eroded over the course of the seventeenth century by a range of adverse factors including: family failure and the lack of heirs; economic pressure and the effect of fines; property losses; the pressure from political events such as the Popish Plot to encourage apostasy; and the effects of such crises as the Civil War.

The Preston family, prime standard-bearers of Furness gentry recusancy, experienced several of the exigencies listed above. Their protection of their faith in our area is evident above all in their creation of a chaplaincy at their estate of the Manor during their residence there between the late 1580s and 1678. There was always at least one priest at the Manor and very often two, some of whose names are known. At some point before 1625, when he became superior of the Lancashire mission, Fr Laurence Anderton, S.J., a Lancashire-born priest,[20] was at the Manor when Agnes, the daughter of

John Preston (died 1643, father to Sir John Preston), married Christopher Anderton, of Lostock Hall, and it is presumed that he spent some of his earlier missionary life at the Manor.[21] John Michell came to the English Mission from Douai on in 1578, and in 1593 was reported, by a spy, as being a priest in Lancashire.[22] He was recorded as one of John Preston's chaplains at the Manor in 1629, but died shortly thereafter. John Sefton,[23] who was chaplain with John Michell, was still at the Manor in 1631.[24]

During the residency of the Prestons, the chaplains at the Manor, with the exception of Laurence Anderton, S.J., were all seminary priests: the next to arrive, John Huddleston,[25] had been educated at Douai and ordained a secular priest but ended his life a Benedictine. According to Gillow, he resided at the Manor, acting as chaplain, between 1637 and 1645.[26] We can, in fact, narrow this down, because Huddleston must have left in either 1642 or 1643, at, or near the beginning of the Civil War. This is evidenced by remarks made by Samuel Pepys after an interview in which John Huddleston admitted that in the earlier months of the war, he 'came in [to the Royalist army] with Sir Jno. Preston under the Duke of Newcastle and continued actually in the war till … the old King was taken'; Blount's Royalist memoir, the *Boscobel Book* (3rd edn, 1680) tells us that Huddleston was 'a gentleman volunteer in his late majesty's service, first under Sir John Preston the Elder till Sir John was rendered unserviceable from the desperate wounds he received in that service at Furness'.[27]

The allusion in that recollection is to the sacrifice that Sir John Preston the elder of the Manor made for the royalist cause in the Civil War. Following the outbreak of the war,[28] along with the Penningtons of Muncaster and the Kirkbys of Kirkby Ireleth, both branches of the Prestons – of the Manor and of Holker – were active in Furness in the king's cause, alongside the Catholic Viscount Molyneux and Sir John Maney.[29] The lesser gentry of the area also aligning themselves with the Royalist cause were the Knipes of Rampside and the Catholic branch of the Rawlinsons of Cark Hall. Sir John Preston was created a baronet for his early Civil War service to the Crown, and whilst in Furness in 1644 was to render further loyal service to the king's cause, when a skirmish, thought to have taken place near Hawcoat, not far from his home the Manor, resulted in a head injury which was the cause of his death the following year.[30]

The death of Sir John Preston, with his son and heir a minor, obviously represented a major setback for the Catholic cause and its gentry leadership in Stuart Furness, but the male line of the Preston family of the Manor of Furness Abbey in fact came to its end with Sir Thomas, third and last baronet, who, on the death of his second wife, and a year after his only son had died, decided in 1673 to spend his remaining years in the service of God and entered the Society of Jesus at Watten in Flanders. He declined ordination, having scruples because he had been twice married, but remained a 'formed-scholastic', taking religious vows and remaining under obedience, until his death in 1709, aged 66, at Watten.[31] On entering the Society, he settled his estates in Westmorland, Northamptonshire and properties at Quernmore in Lancashire on his two infant daughters,[32] at the same time providing funds that made it possible, eventually, for the

Society to allow £20 per annum for the maintenance of a chaplain for the Manor Mission.[33]

In 1678, during the period when the Manor was occupied by Sir Thomas Preston's two daughters, after his departure to Watten, Richard Fletcher, alias Barton, a Douai priest, took up residence there with Nicholas Grimshaw, both acting as chaplains. This coincided with the Titus Oates Plot which arose from, and raised, the anti-popery endemic in seventeenth-century England.[34] Oates claimed, falsely, that a vast Catholic conspiracy existed to assassinate Charles II and, with foreign aid, replace him with his Catholic brother, James Duke of York. With particular reference to our region, Oates insinuated that Fletcher, known by his alias Barton, was involved with this plot and a raid was made on the Manor in the first week of November in an endeavour to arrest the Manor chaplains Fletcher and Grimshaw, but they had left a week before. The staunch Anglican Justice Daniel Fleming of Rydal led the raid and seized all the arms at the Manor.[35] Richard Fletcher evaded arrest until 1679 when he was tried at Lancaster, condemned to death for being a priest, was reprieved and pardoned, but remained a prisoner in Lancaster Castle.[36] There is no record of why he escaped the death penalty; however, increasing public scepticism of the evidence produced by Oates resulted in a series of acquittals from the beginning of July 1679 of Catholics arraigned on treason charges.[37] On his release from gaol on 10 March 1685, following the accession of the Catholic James II in February, Fletcher returned to the Mission in Lancashire: his will of 1700 describes him as of Wood-within-Melling, where he served until his death in 1701. He was buried at Harkirk, Little Crosby.[38] It is thought that Nicholas Grimshaw, the other priest who served at the Manor at the same time as Fletcher/Barton and escaped with him, was probably apprehended and convicted of being a priest when his brother, with whom he may have sought refuge at Clayton Hall, Clayton-le-Woods, Lancashire, was convicted of recusancy in 1679.[39] As nothing further is heard of him, it is presumed that he eventually died in prison. The 1678 raid on the Manor whose purpose was the arrest of Barton and Grimshaw brought to an end the chaplaincy there and Mass ceased to be said at the Manor of Furness.

Indeed, the Oates Plot was devastating for the Prestons of the Manor, as it was for Furness Catholicism and for the gentry leadership of any extant plebeian Catholic remnant, with the simultaneous abandonment of Catholicism by the Kirkbys of Kirkby Ireleth and the Prestons of Holker (though the Bardsey family remained loyal). Not only was the chaplaincy closed down but at this juncture Sir Thomas Preston's distant relative and namesake at Holker conformed, and, on the false charge that Sir Thomas was a Jesuit priest and had settled the Manor estates on the Society, claimed the estate and succeeded, in spite of the prior claims of the Catholic Prestons of Cockerham, in persuading the Crown to confiscate the estates as having been given to 'superstitious uses'.[40] After some years and at great expense, Thomas Preston of Holker persuaded the Crown to grant him, first, a long lease, and, ultimately possession of the whole estate. He died without male issue on 31 January 1696, when the estate passed to his daughter, wife of William Lowther, the Prestons of both Holker and the Manor having become extinct in the male line. William Lowther was created a baronet in 1697, and his grandson, Sir Thomas Lowther, third and last baronet, devised his Holker and Furness estates to his cousins, Lord George Augustus Cavendish (d. 1794), and Lord Frederick Cavendish (d. 1803), younger sons of the third Duke of Devonshire. Holker later descended through the cadet line to Victor Christian William Cavendish (1868–1938), and when he succeeded his uncle as ninth Duke of Devonshire in 1908, it became the property of his younger brother, Lord Richard Frederick Cavendish and has continued in the male line of the Cavendish family to the present day.[41]

At a low point, around the time of the Popish Plot, in the fortunes of Catholicism in Furness, with vital 'seigneurial' patronage rapidly receding, the Manor thus passed out of Catholic hands, though the 'Manor Mission' continued through the forethought of Sir Thomas Preston. Contrary to an accusation made, Thomas had not left his estate to the Society of Jesus; he was, however, responsible for the Jesuits' ability to continue serving what became 'The Manor Mission'. Sir Thomas had secured three small farms, two in the parish of Dalton – Goldmire and Stonedyke – and one in the parish of Urswick – Stainton – which by an ingenious legal stratagem were exempted from the estate which devolved upon the Prestons of Holker. Sir Thomas had ordered some small amounts of money to be paid to certain unknown individuals; these were specified in the 'Articles of Agreement', dated 1677 between the Catholic trustees of the Preston estate: Lord Carrington, Viscount Molyneux, Richard Walmsley and Robert Dalton; but Preston had also secured the three farms with the intention of either selling the real estate or using the income for the foundation of a novitiate for the English Province of the Society of Jesus. That proved impracticable, so the income was diverted to sustain the Manor Mission in Furness. In 1711 the farms were vested in trust for the Society in the name of Lady Catherine Stourton, the widow of Robert, seventh Lord Petre, and daughter and heiress of Bartholomew Walmsley of Dunkenhalgh. In later years the Petre family were responsible for this trust.[42] It was through this legacy that the Jesuits came to serve the Manor Mission and were able to keep the Catholic faith alive in Furness. That patronal role of preservation also involved the lesser gentry family of the Bardseys.

Such provincial recusant families typically combined their Catholic faith with deep loyalty to the Crown; indeed, although throughout the Stuart period, genuine Catholic loyalty was extensively doubted, a typical observation of one Nathaniel West in 1667 to the effect that 'the king has not any subjects that will swear higher allegiance than the Papists will' represented an accurate assessment of the fact that, in spite of scruples preventing their taking the Oath of Allegiance which violated their obedience to the Holy See, the bulk of the Catholic gentry remained loyal to the Crown; for example, in the witchhunt stirred up by Oates' allegations in 1678, the Catholic Sir Thomas Strickland of Sizergh testified in 1679 to the kind of basic loyalty of most English Catholics by informing the justices at Kendal that, although he could not take the oath recognising the king's supremacy in religion, he would 'swear to defend the king against all enemies … and against the pope, no less than against a pagan, should he invade the king's dominions'.[43] The unfounded accusations of Oates provoked a furious political campaign to exclude the Duke of York from the succession. By 1681 this agitation on the part of the newly formed Whig party had been thwarted by Charles II and his Tory allies, and in 1685 the Catholic Duke of York came peaceably to the throne as James II, easing the situation for his co-religionists sufficiently for John Leyburn, the first of the vicars-apostolic,[44] and the first Catholic bishop to function in England for fifty years, to make a confirmation visitation. Bishop Leyburn did not reach Furness in his peregrination: Witherslack, near Kendal was the nearest he came to our area. How many from Furness were included in the list of *confirmandi* at that place, we do not know, but the inclusion of a recognisable gentry surname, a Knipe, may well suggest that recusant squires of our area brought followings of 'plebeian' recusants with them to Witherslack.

By December 1688, James' campaign to end discrimination against Catholics and Nonconformists resulted in his deposition or abdication, and the 'Glorious Revolution' of 1688–9 was set in motion. The anti-Catholic backlash set off by the Revolution, having the inevitable effect of further eroding indispensable gentry patronal support for Catholicism, was fully evident at Bardsey Hall, home of the Catholic Bardsey (or Bardsea) family, which became a centre of worship after the Manor of Furness passed out of Catholic hands in 1678. At the time of the Revolution of 1688, the resident priest at Bardsey was Clement Smith, S.J., and his story, recounted in the Society's Annual Letters for 1688, gives some idea of the life of a Catholic priest in those troubled times.[45] Clement Smith died at Bardsey Hall, on 8 September 1695, and was buried in Urswick church-yard on 16 September. His sufferings, combined with constant anxiety, had undermined his constitution. He was aged thirty-eight when he died, not strictly speaking a martyr, but one of many priests of the penal period who gave their lives for their faith.

The lesser gentry family of the Bardseys had been strong recusants from Elizabethan days. In the 1590s, Richard Bardsey was reported as having 'a flee boat' in which he carried escaping priests to safety in either Scotland or Ireland:[46] this would no doubt be from Piel. Either he or his father must have been the 'ould Bardsey of Furnis who was a great papist', known to the authorities in the 1590s.[47] The last of the male line of the Bardsey family died in 1642 fighting for the royal cause and so the Hall passed in the female line to the Andertons of Clayton Hall, Clayton-le-Woods. In 1655, James Anderton, a recusant and suspected royalist, was living at Bardsey Hall. He died in London in 1676 but his widow Jane, also a recusant, took up residence at Bardsey Hall and was there in 1679. James' brother Christopher inherited and was presumably at Bardsey, probably with his sister-in-law Jane, if she was still alive, and his unmarried sister Mary, and it was they who gave succour to Clement Smith at the cost, according to the law, of forfeiting their lives if they were caught. They, as well as Clement Smith, must have suffered many hours of anxiety while he was living under their roof.

Christopher Anderton died and was buried at Urswick in 1694, the last male representative of his family. Mary inherited Bardsey Hall and another

FIGURE 6.
Kirkby Hall, residence
of the Kirkby family.

sister, Dorothy, joined her there in her widowhood. Mary continued to live
there until 1701, when she sold the Hall to the Catholic Viscount Molyneux;
she retired to Aldcliffe, the home near Lancaster, of the Catholic Daltons,
where she died in 1708–9 and was buried in Lancaster. Viscount Molyneux
used Bardsey as a hunting lodge and was usually accompanied on his visits
by a priest from his seat, Croxteth Hall. One of these priests, Thomas
Worthington, O.P., noted that he celebrated Mass at Bardsey in August
1717.[48] The Hall, after being a Mass centre and a safe house for priests since
the time of the Reformation, was sold in 1732 by the Molyneux family to
Christopher Wilson, of London, and descended, first to the Braddyls, then
the Gales, and thus into Protestant hands. It was demolished earlier this
century. Once more, the case of the Bardsey family illustrates the seemingly
inevitable removal of indispensable gentry support, through lack of male
heirs, from the Furness recusant legacy.

Rampside Hall 'in the township of Yarleside, and the parish of Dalton'
was the home of another lesser gentry recusant family, the Knipes, who
appear on recusant rolls from the beginning of Elizabeth's reign. John Knipe
fought on the side of the king during the Civil War and was killed in the
battle of Brindle Heath on 23 August 1651. Rampside Hall was a refuge for
missionary priests, as was, in the latter half of the seventeenth century, the
home of the Lacey family of Newbarns, in 'the township of Hawcoat', also
in the parish of Dalton.[49] Kirkby Hall, lying within the scattered parish of
Kirkby Ireleth, was another Mass centre where an upper room served as a
chapel. It was the seat of the Kirkby family, but owing to fines imposed
through the Kirkby family's tenacious loyalty to the Royalist cause during
the Civil War, Roger Kirkby mortgaged the whole of his estates, which were
eventually acquired by the Cavendish family. At some time, probably at the
time of the Oates Plot, the Kirkbys conformed, so Kirkby Hall and family
were lost to Catholicism; the Prestons of Holker Hall had also remained

staunch to the old faith until Thomas Preston conformed when he inherited the Manor estates of Furness.[50]

FIGURE 7. Rampside Hall, the residence of the Knipe family. (*Photograph: Angus Winchester*)

With the eventual disappearance of the Catholic gentry families, together with the lack, for a time, of Catholic priests after 1688, Catholicism reached its nadir in Furness. It is not surprising that the majority of the plebeian Catholics began to take the line of least resistance and join their neighbours in attending the local parish church. The parish church had always been the focal point of village life in England and when that church was made over to the Established Church the local people had little option but to conform. As we shall see, a few remained faithful, but they were indeed the 'remnant'.

Notes

1. See Antonia Fraser, *The Gunpowder Plot* (London: Weidenfeld & Nicolson, 1996).
2. 3. Jac. I c. 5. An act to prevent and avoid dangers which grow by popish recusants: see B. C. Foley, *Some Other People of the Penal Times* (Preston: Snape & Co., 1991), Appendix 1, 'The First of Five Repressive Acts of James I' (Extracts), pp. 156–9.
3. J. A. Hilton, 'The Cumbrian Catholics', *Northern History*, vol. 16 (1980), p. 48.
4. B. G. Blackwood, in 'Plebeian Catholics in the 1640s and 1650s', *Recusant History*, vol. 18, no. 1 (1986), p. 46; Table 1: 'Gentry and Plebeian Catholics in 1641' shows that 93% of Lancashire Catholics can be identified as 'plebeian' (non-gentry or -noble), as against 7% gentry, p. 51.
5. Haigh, *Reformation and Resistance*, p. 244.

6. See above chapter 1, n. 15.

7. *VCH Lancs*, vol. 8, p. 302 n. 113; *Camden Misc.*, Camden Soc., ix, 80.

8. *VCH Lancs*, vol. 8, p. 303 n. 114.

9. CRS, *Misc.*, iv, pp. 163–4.

10. Barnes, *Barrow and District*, p. 70. For influence of wives in Catholic households see John Bossy, *The English Catholic Community 1570–1850* (London: Darton, Longman & Todd, 1975), pp. 153–4; Hilton 'The Cumbrian Catholics', *Northern History*, vol. 16, p. 46.

11. CRS, *Lancashire Registers, III, North Part.* vol. 20 (1916), p. 3.

12. *VCH Lancs*, vol. 8, p. 303, n. 114.

13. CRS, *Recusant Rolls 2, 1593–94*, vol. 57 (1965).

14. CRS, 61, *Recusant Rolls 3–4 1595–96 (1970)*, 'Scales' is a village adjacent to Newton, between Urswick and Aldingham.

15. *VCH Lancs*, vol. 8, p. 303.

16. Blackwood, 'Plebeian Catholics', *Recusant History*, Table 3: 'Lancashire Catholics in 1651: A Social Analysis', p. 52.

17. Barnes, *Barrow and District*, p. 58.

18. These figures are estimated from John Bossy, *The English Catholic Community 1570–1850* (London: Darton, Longman & Todd, 1975), Map 1: Distribution of Catholics, 1641–42, p. 404.

19. *VCH Lancs*, vol. 8, p. 326, n. 63.

20. Thomas M. McCoog, *English and Welsh Jesuits 1555–1650*, CRS, vol. 74 (1994), p. 103.

21. CRS, vol. 16, p. 421; CRS, *Lancashire Registers*, p. 4.

22. PRO SP. 12 Dom. Eliz. 33, n. 64; CRS, *Lancashire Registers*, p. 4.

23. Godfrey Anstruther, *The Seminary Priests, 1558–1659* (4 vols, Great Wakering: Mayhew–McCrimmon, 1968–77, vol. 2, p. 274.

24. CRS, *Lancashire Registers*, p. 4.

25. Anstruther, *The Seminary Priests*, vol. 2, p. 163; A. F. Allison and D. M. Rogers, 'Biographical Studies, 1534–1829', *Recusant History*, vol. 1 (1951–2), p. 257; see Appendix 2.

26. CRS, *Lancashire Registers*, p. 4.

27. Allison and Rogers, 'Biographical Studies', pp. 254–5.

28. For the civil war in the region, see Ernest Broxap, *The Great Civil War in Lancashire (1642–1651)* (Manchester: Manchester University Press, 2nd edn, 1973).

29. Barnes, *Barrow and District* pp. 59–66. For Catholic Royalism see: B. G. Blackwood, *The Lancashire Gentry and the Great Rebellion*, Chetham Society, 3rd series, vol. 25 (1978);and P. R. Newman, 'Roman Catholic Royalists-Papist Commanders, 1642–1680', *Recusant History*, vol. 15, no. 6 (1981), pp. 396–405.

30. CRS, *Lancashire Registers*, p. 4.

31. Foley, *Records of the English Province of the Society of Jesus*, vol. 7, p. 631.

32. CRS, *Lancashire Registers*, p. 2.

33. Ibid., pp. 3, 8.

34. For these events see John Kenyon, *The Popish Plot* (London: Heinemann, 1972), and Michael Mullett, *James II and English Politics* (London: Routledge, 1994), pp 5–12; for anti-popery, see John Miller, *Popery and Politics in England, 1660–1688* (London: Cambridge University Press, 1973).

35. PRO S.P. Dom., Charles II, p. 45, n. 411.

36. M. A. Tierny (ed.), *Dodd's, Church History of England from the commencement of the 16th century to the Revolution in 1688* (5 vols, Wolverhampton: 1737–42), vol. 3, p. 400.

37. J. P. Kenyon, *Stuart England*, 2nd edn (London: Penguin Books, 1985), p. 231.

38. Anstruther, *The Seminary Priests*, vol. 2, pp. 113–114.

39. CRS, *Lancashire Registers*, p. 6.

40. Danby Pickering (ed.), *Statutes at Large*, 30 Car.2, cap. 2 (London: Cambridge University Press, 1778), vol. 10, pp. 315–19.

41. CRS, *Lancashire Registers*, p. 2; R. S. Boumphrey, C. Roy Hudleston and J. Hughes, *An Armorial For Westmorland and Lonsdale*, CW Extra Series, vol. 21 (1975), pp. 69–70.

42. CRS, *Lancashire Registers*, p. 3. For background to Lady Stourton see B. C. Foley, 'Catherine Walmsley' (1698–1785), in *Some Other People of the Penal Times*, pp. 1–22.

43. Historical MSS. Commission Report: MSS of Le Fleming (London: HMSO, 1890), pp. 44–154, quoted in Bouch and Jones, *Short History of the Lake Counties*, p. 175.

44. A vicar apostolic was a titular bishop answerable directly to the Holy See and without chapter or diocese.

45. Foley, *Records S.J.*, vol 5, Ser. 12, pp 353–358. For full account of Clement Smith in Furness, see Appendix 1.

46. CRS, *English Martyrs*, 1, p. 180–1.

47. See above Chapter 3, n. 32.

48. CRS, *Lancashire Registers*, p. 7.

49. Ibid., p. 8.

50. Ibid., p. 1, p. 2.

CHAPTER FIVE

Penal times – 'The long eighteenth century'

The Revolution witnessed an inevitable upsurge of anti-popery and new anti-Catholic legislation followed. Under the Act of 1700,[1] 'for the further preventing the growth of popery' a reward of £100 was offered to anyone apprehending a 'popish bishop, priest or jesuit'. The punishment targeted any 'popish bishop, priest or jesuit ... who was convicted of saying mass, or any person ... making profession of the popish religion [who] shall keep school ...' and it was enacted that 'every such person shall on such conviction be adjudged to perpetual imprisonment'. The same statute reiterated an earlier act, of Charles II,[2] passed at the height of the Popish Plot scare, whereby a Catholic was made incapable of inheriting lands but 'the next of his or her kindred, which shall be protestant, shall have and enjoy the said lands'. The Act of Settlement of 1701 reiterated the exclusion of Catholics from succeeding to the throne and from royal marriages, as well as paving the way for the eventual succession of the Protestant House of Hanover. Despite such legislation, as we shall see, the eighteenth century saw a gradual relaxation both of official repression and, slowly, of public mistrust.[3]

In Furness, following the death in 1695 of the first priest to be sent to serve the Manor Mission, Clement Smith, the next priest to be recorded, in 1701 and again in 1704, was William Gardner, alias Taylor, S.J.[4] On 2 October 1716, when he was convicted of recusancy at the Lancaster Sessions, he was residing in the parish of Pennington, near Ulverston.[5] The aftermath of the Jacobite rising of 1715, in which Catholics in general were deemed to be implicated in a bid to place James II's Catholic son James Edward on the throne, displacing the Hanoverian succession, resulted in the implementation of An Act to oblige Papists to register their Names and real Estates;[6] this was followed in 1716 by an Act for the purpose of 'appointing Commissioners to enquire of the Estates of certain Traitors [Jacobites], and Popish Recusants, and of Estates given to superstitious Uses, in order to raise Money out of them severally for the Use of the Publick'.[7] Such estates were forfeit to the Crown and the farms of the Preston Estate in Furness in trust for the Jesuits were now at serious risk of confiscation owing to Gardner's incarceration, if it could be proved that he, a convicted recusant, owned them. The gravity of the situation for local Catholics following 1715 is apparent from the fact that four other priests, presumably from Lancashire, were arrested with Gardner and all convicted of either recusancy or of being priests and imprisoned in Lancaster Castle, even though they were all soon released. Another, James Swarbrick, was arrested, convicted, but remained imprisoned at Lancaster, where he died in 1716.[8]

The economic situation of the whole of the Catholic community was indeed in jeopardy through the work of the Forfeited Estates Commission; however, many legal subterfuges prevented what might well have been utter catastrophe. In many cases sympathetic Protestants would take possession of land, acting as temporary trustees in such a way as to make it extremely difficult for the Estates Commissioners to ascertain who was the rightful owner of the land in question.[9] The original safeguards taken by the trustees of the Preston estate in 1677 were now to prove their worth. What came to the attention of the authorities was the mechanism – a complex one – by which William Gardner/Taylor derived his income from rents of the farms. The High Constable for Lonsdale North of the Sands reported on 2 October 1716:

> An estate of Mr Taylor, a suspected Romish Priest lying att Stone dikes in the sd Townpp [the township of Leece, in the parish of Aldingham] valued att £12 p.an. The personall estate of the sd Mr Taylor in the townpp of Pennington, where he resides, valued at £08.00.00. An estate called Goldmire lying near Dalton in the sd co. heretofore lett by one Geo. Kemp, steward or servt to Sir Nicholas Sherburn for the sum of £6 p.an. & supposed to be to the use of the sd Mr Taylor. A pcell of ground now farmed by one Thos. Brigg of Holbeck at £3 p.an, the rent supposed to be to the use of the sd Mr Taylor.[10]

There is further information from the same source, dated 20 November 1716, 'that Thomas Briggs and Thomas Browne of Dalton-in-Furness pay rent to Mary Richardson (for lands in Dalton) to one Taylor a priest'.[11] Despite the various legal stratagems that had been constructed to conceal their purpose of sustaining the Catholic mission, the Estates Commissioners must have had strong suspicions about these Furness farms. Even so, they escaped forfeiture: perhaps the original legal arrangements were too complex and the authorities were simply unable to prove who was the rightful owner; or the Commissioners considered the estate too small to warrant their attention; or the examiners, although Protestant, were sympathetic to the Catholics and did not wish to see their neighbours subjected to excessively stringent measures.[12] William Gardner now returned from Lancaster Castle, in late 1716, settled in Dalton and lived there until his death on 1 April 1725, aged 74 years.[13]

William Gardner's death was followed by a period without a resident priest in Furness, and the area was served by itinerants, known as 'riding priests', who covered the Kendal, Workington and Furness districts. One was a Benedictine, Dom William Bede Hutton, ordained in 1720, who, after serving the Benedictines' Northern Province at Stella, near Newcastle, was transferred in 1735 to Kendal, possibly at the home of the Catholic gentry family of Strickland, Sizergh Castle, which was his base until 1747. During these twelve years the rents from the three farms were sent to the English Provincial of the Society of Jesus who remitted them to the regional Benedictine superior, one Naylor, to cover the expenses of Dom William Bede during his intermittent visits to Furness. The farms, held in trust by the Catholic Lady Stourton, widow of Robert, seventh Lord Petre, were administered by her agent Mr Chadwick, who, in his Furness accounts for 1742, recorded the payments:

> Oct. 13th By paid Mr Naylor for Mr Hutton for assisting at Lindell 2 years, 1741 and 1742 ... £16.16.0. By John Brewer for use of his House for Prayers [Mass] for 2 years ... £2.2.0.

In the years 1749 and 1753, Chadwick's accounts also recorded reimbursements to a Mr Hunter, a Jesuit and a 'riding priest' based at Sizergh who received annually eight guineas, while John Brewer continued to receive the sum of £1 1s. (a guinea) for the use of his house. From 1749 to 1753 the visiting priest was a Mr Skelton who travelled from Lancaster across the sands to serve Furness. The amount paid to him was ten guineas and the steadfast Brewer continued to make his house available for Mass for the usual guinea.[14]

The next priest serving the Manor Mission of whom we have record is William Strickland, S.J., who was appointed on his ordination in 1759, appropriately enough, as chaplain at his family home, Sizergh Castle, from which base he served the Catholics in Furness, receiving for his services ten guineas a year. Subsequently Strickland became chaplain to the Catholic Weld family at Stonyhurst, Lancashire.[15] In 1593 the Society of Jesus had founded a college at St Omer (then in Flanders but subsequently taken into France), for the education of English Catholic boys, but in 1762 they were forced by the French government to leave, taking refuge in Bruges in the Catholic, Austrian-ruled Netherlands. In 1773, the Society of Jesus was suppressed by Pope Clement XIV, a measure imposed on him by various European sovereigns. No charges were proved against the Jesuits and in fact they survived in Russia owing to the refusal of Catherine the Great (1729–96) to promulgate the papal brief. After their suppression the Jesuits, masters and boys, moved gradually in the autumn and early winter of 1773, from Bruges to their college at Liège in the southern Netherlands, where the now ex-Jesuits continued to study.[16] It was to this academy that William Strickland was invited by the staff as president in June or July 1784,[17] and it was he who supervised its further evacuation, this time before the advance of the French Revolutionary army into the southern Netherlands, to Stonyhurst in Lancashire, given in 1794 to the Jesuits by the Weld family. While at Liège, Strickland was given the extra responsibility of administrator and, in effect, leader of the English disbanded Jesuits, controlling and husbanding their resources in the hope that the Society would one day be restored. It was due to his acumen that, when this restoration did occur, in 1814, the English Province of the Society was in a better position than had been thought possible. Stonyhurst[18] retained the Liège academy's status of a pontifical college, and on this basis was partially exempt from the jurisdiction of the Vicar Apostolic of the Northern District. William Strickland maintained a close connection with Stonyhurst, and also had oversight of the accounts of the Manor Mission.[19] As we shall see, he was to be instrumental in securing a priest – one of considerable distinction – for Ulverston in 1794.

Despite the enactment of new penal laws, and the retention on the statute book of the older recusancy legislation, as the eighteenth century progressed the feeling against Catholics eased in some, especially more educated, circles, and it was felt by many that the laws, especially the restriction on inheritance by Catholics under the Act 30 Car. 2, cap. 2, reiterated in Guil. III, cap. 4 were unjust. The particular laws making Catholics incapable of inheriting estates whose ownership had to be transferred to Protestant relations were challenged by Ann Fenwick of Hornby, the sole heiress of her father's fortune, who, when widowed in 1757, was stripped of her inheritance from her husband's estate by her brother-in-law who claimed the right to it under the Act of 1700, because he was a Protestant and she a Catholic. Ann's wealthy Catholic parents, Thomas and Ann Benison, had built a large mansion, Town End Hall, Hornby. When her father died in 1735, Ann being only eleven years old, the estate was left in trust to her and administered by her mother and another trustee until she came of age. She subsequently married John Fenwick, a Protestant, in 1752, and on her marriage allowed her income to be added temporarily to her husband's so as to assist in a business transaction. John died suddenly after only five years of marriage, before he could restore her inheritance, at which point Ann's Protestant brother-in-law, Thomas Fenwick, claimed legal entitlement to her estate, leaving Ann penniless. It was only in response to local outcry that Thomas Fenwick agreed to allow Ann to continue to live at Town End Hall and to pay her a small annuity. The subsequent failure of Thomas to honour these arrangements led to a *cause célèbre*. In 1770, Ann's plight was brought to the notice of Lord Camden, the Lord Chancellor, and in 1772 he was successful in bringing a private Act of Parliament to provide some remedy in her case. She received an increased annuity and a lump sum in cash.

Ann Fenwick's case aroused the conscience of much of the nation as a result of speeches by Lord Camden in the House of Lords and by Edmund Burke, after the outcome of the Fenwick case, to his constituents at Bristol in 1772.[20] This case revealed the general feeling both within and without Parliament that relaxation of the harsh penal laws was desirable. The government was favourable to change, though it stipulated that an Oath of Allegiance to George III was essential, whereupon a group of Catholic nobility and gentry started to move in the matter. Robert Edward, ninth Lord Petre (grand-son of Lady Stourton), led the group in discussions with the government and the Vicars Apostolic to formulate an oath that would be acceptable for Catholics to take.[21] After much patient negotiation, agreement was reached which bore fruit with the eventual passing of the two Relief Acts of 1778 and 1791:[22] the first freed Catholics from legal disabilities and persecution liable under the William III 1700 Act against Popery: priests were no longer threatened with life imprisonment and the £100 reward to informers was dispensed with; even so, the offence of recusancy still remained on the statute book and prosecutions could, and did follow non-attendance at Anglican services. The 1778 Relief Act, by lifting the prohibitions on priests imposed by the legislation of 1700, made *de jure*, what, through a reluctance to prosecute, had come to be *de facto* freedom of worship. The 1778 Relief Act paved the way for the official freedom of worship provided by the second Relief Act of 1791.

It was during this more tolerant period of the later eighteenth century

FIGURE 8.
Titeup Hall, first
lodging in Furness of
Thomas West, S.J.
(*Photograph: Angus
Winchester*)

that one of the most famous of the Manor Mission priests, Thomas West,
S.J., came to Furness. Born, apparently, Thomas Daniel, in Inverness at
some point between 1716 and 1720, he received his early education at the
'public schools' of Edinburgh, so one can presume that his parents were
not Catholic, and that at some subsequent point he became a convert to
Catholicism. Daniel spent some time as a 'mercantile traveller', which may
have involved travel on the Continent. On deciding to join the Society of
Jesus, he entered the novitiate of the English province at Watten in 1751,
from where he moved to Liège, prior to his ordination in 1757; at or shortly
after which point he followed the usual British Jesuit concealment strategy
of adopting an alias, in this case 'West'. Like other Georgian Scots Catholic
clergy, above all Thomas Innes,[23] West developed an interest in antiquities

and was elected to the Society of Antiquaries in 1752, when he was a Jesuit novice. Fr West began his missionary work in England in 1758, the year following his ordination, but in 1763 returned to Watten. It is likely that he returned to England in 1765 or early 1766, upon his appointment to the Manor Mission of Furness. He took up residence at Titeup Hall, near Dalton, owned by the Matson family, local ironmasters, not known Catholics, but at the very least sympathetic, who provided him with rent-free lodging.[24]

Thomas West's first published work as an historian was *The Antiquities of Furness or An Account of the Royal Abbey of St Mary*, published in 1774, and dedicated to 'The Right Honourable Lord George Cavendish, First Uncle to His Grace the Duke of Devonshire' of Holker Hall. *An Account of Antiquities Discovered in Lancaster*, followed in 1776, and his best known book, *A Guide to the Lakes*, in 1778. In *The Antiquities*, West made particularly favourable comments on the inhabitants of his adopted district:

> The people of Furness in general and of Ulverston in particular are civil and well behaved; to strangers hospitable and humane ... The modesty of the female sex and sobriety of the men prevent irregularities before marriage and secure conjugal love and affection through life.[25]

This admiration for Furness people was reciprocated, and West enjoyed a particular friendship with the Cavendish family at Holker. Lord George Cavendish, in whose possession Furness Abbey by then rested, offered the use of the crypt for Catholic worship, but the priest did not think it would be prudent to take up the offer, even though by that time people in general were becoming more tolerant.[26] However, the people of Furness, and visitors more generally, have Thomas West's friendship with Lord George Cavendish to thank for persuading him to prevent further damage to, and so preserve, the magnificent ruins of the Abbey.[27] Fr West was also on friendly terms with Edward Jackson, Vicar of Colton north of Ulverston, who in a diary entry gave West his Jesuit priest's title: 'June 25th, 1775, Breakfast with Father West'[28] Thomas West's friendship with Lord George Cavendish and the Vicar of Colton, can be compared with that of John Lingard's amiable relationship, while priest at Hornby, with the parson and the squire of that place.[29] Although West had spent ten years in what he considered 'the best house in Low Furness',[30] Titeup Hall, it would seem that his health was troubling him, so that a friend, James Collinson, of Lancaster, being concerned for Fr West, wrote to him 21 November 1775:

> I suppose you intend to winter at Titeup, which is but a cold and bleak situation far from society. If you could meet with convenient lodgings at Ulverston which is at no great distance, and stay there for two or three of these dark months, it would in my opinion be far more comfortable.[31]

It would appear that Fr West heeded this advice and took lodgings in 1776, at Swarthmoor Hall, near Ulverston, better known for its connections with George Fox, the Quaker founder; there he said Mass regularly over a period of about twelve months.[32]

West's move to Swarthmoor Hall may need some explanation: the

Elizabethan hall was sold in 1759 by the Fell family, descendants of George Fox's second wife, Margaret Fell, by her first marriage; however, its purchaser, Captain Lindow, had allowed the property to fall into a state of disrepair, only part being habitable, and that occupied by a tenant farmer.[33] This situation raises the questions: was the tenant farmer a Catholic? Likewise was Captain Lindow?: the answer would seem to be in the affirmative if he was a member of the Ulverston Lindow family, one of whose members, John, was a secular priest and a correspondent of Thomas West.[34] In that case, Lindow's patronage and the move of the Furness Catholic centre of activity closer towards the market town of Ulverston can be viewed as symptomatic of a key shift taking place in the whole orientation of north-western recusancy in the course of the eighteenth century – a move away from rural gentry manor houses (such as Sizergh Castle) and towards the vicinities of the new urban foci of Georgian Catholicism, where, at fairly short distances from towns such as Kendal (with Dodding Green) and Preston (with Fernyhalgh), informal Mass centres grew up to serve urban (as well as still relatively numerous rural) Catholic worshippers. It was outside Ulverston too, that, in 1688, George Fox had provided the Quakers with the Meeting House of Swarthmore, where, over a period of months long-established Quaker meetings for worship co-existed in close proximity to Fr West's celebrations of Mass at the Hall.

It may seem strange that Quakers and Catholics should worship in such neighbourliness in this way and that the house in which George Fox had once lived should become a Mass centre. However, this is not as strange or as unusual as it may seem, and certainly not in this period when Quakers and Catholics were in fact growing side-by-side, as is evidenced, for example, in Cleveland and in Upper Yorkshire where they lived amicably together. The Catholic Blundell family of Crosby give us an example of an eirenical attitude. In 1665, William Blundell was enquiring into the religious thinking of his Quaker neighbours; by 1710 his grandson, Nicholas was so interested in the Society of Friends, that he 'went to Liverpool in expectation to have seen a great meeting of Quakers'; though he arrived too late on that occasion, he eventually succeeded in attending a meeting in London.[35] Indeed, there was some affinity between the Catholics and the Society of Friends: the importance members of both communities placed on friendship and aspects of their spirituality and even of their theologies of salvation, based in part on free-will and 'good works' bound them together; both communities were 'Dissenters' and both refused to take oaths required by the law.[36]

Thomas West's sojourn at Swarthmoor was brief; probably owing to the dilapidated conditions prevailing at Swarthmoor Hall, he moved in the following year to Ulverston and rented what was known as the 'First House' in Fountain Street, Ulverston, but by 1779 he had vacated this house, and his address was by this date a house in the 'Ellers', a street in Ulverston,[37] in effect transferring the Manor Mission there; the house evidently had sufficient room for the celebration of Mass. Father West's priestly ministry in Furness witnessed a recovery in Catholic numbers from a low point at the beginning of the eighteenth century, when, in 1705, the Returns of Papists for the Diocese of Chester showed only one Catholic in the parish of Aldingham: William Hilton and two children, with an annual income of £3, while in Dalton there were only John Blundal, a gentleman worth £40 per annum, with his wife and a few young children; there were also a widow Preston and one Ellen, simply described as 'poor'. In all, this amounts to only five adults in the whole of Furness – not surprising given the long years of persecution that indeed still partially prevailed. However, from the time that Thomas West came to Furness, the number of identifiable Catholics in the area was, without any doubt, increasing, stimulated by iron mining and Irish immigration: in 1767, just a year after West's arrival twenty-one Catholic adults and fourteen children were included in the Return to the House of Lords for Dalton and Ulverston.[38] The occupation for most of the men was given as 'works at ye iron ore Pits'. Thomas West himself wrote, soon after his arrival, that 'The people I wait upon are a few poor paddies from Cork employed here at the iron mines; two farmers came to settle and more are expected'.[39] As only one farmer is listed in the Returns, and he had lived at Dalton for three years, one wonders if the two farmers that Thomas West mentions came later or had escaped being recorded.

Further increase in the Catholic population is evidenced in a letter received by West from a secular priest friend, John Lindow,[40] of the Ulverston family, dated 4 September 1778. This was obviously in reply to one sent by West in which he had suggested that Lindow might buy a house in Soutergate, Ulverston, where he, West could be the tenant. Lindow wrote:

> I thank you for your kind favour of the 25th ult ... I remember seeing the house in Soutergate you speak of, but never was in it. I like the situation, because I think it stands upon hard dry soil. But you make no mention of any land belonging to it; and if there is not any it must be a good house and well furnished to be worth £450 in Ulverstone.
>
> But as for asking me to purchase it, in order for you to be my tenant, I cannot consider this in any other light than a friendly compliment. You say nothing of that separate building you design for the Chapel ...[41]

Clearly, there had been some discussion of what John Lindow referred to as 'that separate building you design for the Chapel'. Though Mass in private houses, while not officially permitted by the first Relief Act, was now, through the impediments on prosecuting priests, in effect accepted practice, the two priests, in any discussion they were having of a 'separate ... Chapel', were anticipating the further change in the law that was to come in 1791. Evidently, rapid increases in the number of Catholics locally focused attention on such prospects, but any proposals for a chapel were put in abeyance with the death of Thomas West at Sizergh Castle, on 10 July, 1779, aged 62, only a few months after receipt of the letter from John Lindow. He was buried, at his own request, just outside the door of the pre-Reformation Sizergh chantry chapel in Kendal parish church. Thomas West's successor was John Sale, S.J., who came to Ulverston at some point in either 1780 or 1781 and died on October 3rd 1791. Little is known of Fr Sale's ministry during these ten or so years. After his death, Dr Rigby, the eminent priest of Lancaster, who worked hard in that mission and raised sufficient money to acquire the premises in Dalton Square, Lancaster for the church there, found time occasionally to assist the Catholics in Ulverston, for which he was paid from the rent from the lands of the Preston legacy.[42]

Thomas West lived long enough to see both the suppression of his Society of Jesus in 1773 and the First Catholic Relief Act in 1778. The Second Catholic Relief Act in 1791 followed the outbreak of the French Revolution, as a result of which many of the French aristocracy, clergy and religious flocked to England for succour. The sympathy of the English people went out to these refugees, and as they were Catholics, some of this sympathy rubbed off on to their English co-religionists.[43] Wordsworth encapsulates the scene in the following sonnet.

> Even while I speak, the sacred roofs of France
> Are shattered into dust; and self-exiled
> From altars threatened, levelled, or defiled,
> Wander the Ministers of God, as chance
> Opens a way for life, or consonance
> Of faith invites. More welcome to no land
> The fugitives than to the British strand,
> Where priest and layman with the vigilance
> Of true compassion greet them. Creed and test
> Vanish before the unreserved embrace
> Of catholic humanity:—*distrest*
> *They came,*—and, while the moral tempest roars
> Throughout the Country they have left, our shores
> Give to their Faith a fearless resting-place.[44]

Under the 1791 Act Catholic worship was now officially allowed and 'chapels' could be built, as long as they did not look like churches: there was to be no spire or tower from which a bell could be rung (though Masses were sometimes timed to coincide with the Anglican services, using the sound of parish church bells to summon the Catholic faithful to Mass). Amidst the sudden influx of priests from France came the Very Rev. Patrick Everard, D. D., Rector of the Irish College, Bordeaux, and administrator of that diocese, an eminent theologian. The Rev. Thomas Allan, in his *Dr Everard, a Memoir*, records the priest's passage through London on his flight from France. There he was introduced to Edmund Burke, who became his friend and introduced him to the leading statesmen and principal Catholics of England; one of these, Fr Allan recalled, was 'the superior of the "gentlemen of the ex-Society"', William Strickland of Sizergh, who immediately invited Dr Everard to serve the Manor Mission now based at Ulverston.[45]

We do not have any evidence of John Sale's address in Ulverston, or whether up to the time of his death in 1791 he continued with the tenancy of the house in the 'Ellers' or not; but even if he did continue to reside in this house, the tenancy must have lapsed on his death, since Dr Rigby was visiting Ulverston on only an intermittent basis, and his occasional visits required no permanent accommodation. All we know is that when Dr Everard arrived in the town in 1794 he complained that 'there was no chapel or house for the priest',[46] so he set about rectifying this deficiency. After

Catholic Church & Presbytery, Ulverston.

the death of Lady Stourton, at the age of 88 in 1785, her grandson, Lord Petre, became her heir-at-law and was responsible for the land left in trust for the Jesuits from Sir Thomas Preston's estate. Dr Everard successfully applied to Lord Petre for permission to sell part of the land, and with the proceeds Everard bought a house, the conveyance being signed by Lord

FIGURE 11.
Datestone on first
Catholic school,
Tarnside, Ulverston.
(*Photograph: Angus
Winchester*)

Petre and Dr Everard 'by the order of Mr [William] Strickland'. Permission
of the Society of Jesus was needed before this transaction could be completed, but there seems to have been some doubt as to whether the lands
left by Sir Thomas Preston belonged entirely to the English Provincial or
to the College of St Aloysius, the Lancashire district of the Society, based
at Stonyhurst. The house that Everard bought in Fountain Street, Ulverston,
appears to have been the same one that Thomas West had rented, 'The
First House', Fountain Street. The house and appurtenances cost £800 and
the balance from the sale of two farms sold was put into the Jesuit trust
funds.[47] The historian Joseph Gillow speculated that Everard extended this
house, and this seems quite possible, because the building was later split
into two residences. It was the first house, coming from the direction of
Lancaster, of a Georgian terrace which now consists of four houses.[48] Dr
Everard was evidently a man of considerable independent means. Although
£800 from the Trust was used to buy the house in Fountain Street, he had
made further private purchases of land which ultimately became the
property of the Society of Jesus.[49]

Dr Everard continued and expanded his predecessor's work, building
on it so as to initiate a Catholic school in Ulverston. This institution was
established in his own house and intended for the sons of better-off
Catholics from as far away as Lytham and Sizergh. The annual 'pension'
paid for these young gentlemen ranged from £200 to £400 each, depending
on their parents' means and the amenities required. There were about
twenty in number and they kept their own horses and dogs. They followed
the hounds, dined, danced, went to card parties[50] and generally followed
the traditional leisured life of Catholic country gentlemen, accompanied
by the doctor himself on these occasions. At first, Dr Everard used a room
in his house as a chapel but soon, in 1806, erected a small one adjoining
the house, dedicating it to Our Lady.[51]

Although, as is evidenced by the passing of the two Catholic Relief Acts,
tolerance towards Catholics was growing, certainly in upper class circles,

there was still a hard core of those who disliked anything or anyone that smacked of 'popery'. This had been amply demonstrated in the ferocious 1780 London Gordon Riot, a mob protest against the 1778 Relief Act. Prejudice was especially evident annually on 5 November, providing an opportunity for some people of Ulverston to vent feelings of bigotry. Dr Everard suffered his share of trouble on these occasions. Guy Fawkes' night would find him behind closed inner shutters and there was a regular order placed with the glazier to call round on 6 November to repair broken windows. However, come Christmas – at least according to Everard's admiring biographer Thomas Allan – generous gifts of food and fuel were sent to his persecutors, by this true Christian gentleman.[52]

FIGURE 12.
Dr Patrick Everard.
(*By kind permission of Leo Warren*)

Dr Everard officially left Ulverston in 1810, when he was elected president of the new Irish seminary at Maynooth. He was by then fifty-eight years old and not in good health, so his stay in Maynooth was never continuous: in fact, he was back in Ulverston recuperating in the same year as his installation and returned time and time again to the town to which he clearly had a great attachment, and especially for his school. His fondness for the locality is evidenced by the fact that in January 1815 he resigned his Maynooth presidency and returned to teach in Ulverston. However, Dr Everard was not allowed to remain in peace there, for the following year he was elected coadjutor to the Archbishop of Cashel, with the right of succession. On the death of Archbishop Bray in 1820, he assumed the position of archbishop in December of that year, but was not destined to exercise his oversight for long, dying only three months later, in March 1821.[53]

The responsibility for the mission at Ulverston, being the natural successor to the Manor Mission, fell on the Society of Jesus, whose nearest house was Stonyhurst. The Society, restored by Pope Pius VII in 1814, was now once more in a position to act with full authority. Fr Stone, the rector of Stonyhurst, sent as successor to Dr Everard an American Jesuit, Nicholas Sewell, who continued as nominal rector of Ulverston for some years, even after his election as rector of Stonyhurst in September 1816. When Fr, or 'Mr', Sewell, as English priests were normally styled at this time, came to Ulverston he found the financial situation less than satisfactory. The farm at Stainton, which was the land remaining from the Preston estate, had been let to a bad farmer who never paid his rent.[54] Fr Sewell sold this land for £2,400 which he reinvested. The sum of £2,000 was lent to Sir Henry Hoghton, of Walton Hall, near Preston, and £400 to the freeholders of Longton at five per cent,[55] but as Sewell wrote to Fr Stone at Stonyhurst, 'on the great fall of interest of money, I reduced the interest of the money lent to Longton to 4 and half per cent'.[56]

After his election as rector of Stonyhurst, Nicholas Sewell remained in nominal charge of the Ulverston mission, keeping it under Jesuit supervision, but found that he needed what would be in effect a replacement and invited a secular priest who had come over from Ireland as an assistant priest in Liverpool, Bartholomew McHugh, to act as *locum tenens*. McHugh soon realised that the building of a proper chapel was imperative, even though the only funds available were from the capital realised from the Stainton farm, the last remnant of the Preston legacy. It was felt that the most sensible thing to do was to realise this money, which had been invested, and this was done. Thereupon, Mr McHugh built his new chapel, in the early neo-gothic style, adjacent to the 'First House' on the corner of Fountain Street and Tarnside. To comply with the restrictions of the 1791 Act, there was no tower, this being added in a castellated style at a later date following the 1829 Catholic Emancipation Act which relaxed the restrictions in the 1791 Relief Act. The first stone was laid on June 27th 1822 and dedicated to St Mary of Furness. An inscription in Latin composed by Mr McHugh stated that the foundation stones were brought from the ruins of Furness Abbey; the ceiling of the chapel is an exact replica of the roof of the building still standing at the southern end of the Abbey ruins, the

Infirmary chapel. Thus, while a link in stone connected the old Abbey with the re-establishment of Catholicism in Furness, the money from the last residue of Sir Thomas Preston's legacy went, eventually, to build the new chapel in the town: he would, surely, rest content to know that he had been the means by which the old faith had been kept alive and was now more openly restored in Furness.

Apart from the work with his flock in Ulverston, Fr McHugh's endeavours and pastoral zeal drove him to extended the limits of the Catholic mission further north into the Furness Peninsula. This drew down on him the wrath of the violently anti-Catholic rector of Aldingham, the reverend John Stonard. Fr McHugh had, it would appear, established a Mass-centre in the area of Haverthwaite, near Newby Bridge and Lakeside, which caused Mr Stonard such concern that he wrote to the bishop of Chester in 1821, asking for a Church of England chapelry to be established in the Haverthwaite area:

> The parish priest of Ulverston is bold as well as assiduous in disseminating the bad seed of his church's superstition … the Romanists at Ulverston are very small … Hence Mr McKew [McHugh] has lately turned his attention to the district above mentioned … he has now a congregation of twenty and he gives them so much of his time, and labours so hard in making additions to them as to cause some murmurs among his people at Ulverston, as being comparatively neglected.[57]

Although pockets of anti-Catholic feeling were to persist throughout the nineteenth century, they were becoming more rare, making the attitude of the rector of Aldingham all the more conspicuous. The friendship of Lord George Cavendish with Fr West in the 1770s had laid the foundations of cordial relations between Catholics and local nobility and gentry in the late eighteenth century; so much so, that in 1830, John Stonard's ire was once again raised, prompting him to write an open letter, disseminated in the form of a printed leaflet, addressed to the local parliamentary candidate, John Wilson Patten, deploring his apparent pro-Catholic tendencies. Among other objections Stonard complained that he had seen Patten walking in Ulverston 'arm-in-arm with the bitterest enemy of the Protestant cause in this part of the country',[Fr McHugh?] and he gave notice that his suspicions had been aroused on learning that the candidate had received hospitality from Lord George Cavendish of Holker and Mr Gale of Bardsey, both known to be sympathetic to Catholics. Stonard's hostility had been fed by the passing, in the previous year, of the Catholic Emancipation Act, about which he complained in his open letter:

> I do not speak entirely as an individual, but as the Rector of a parish, having a character for consistency to uphold with my parishioners. Now I should really be ashamed to look them in the face, were I to give you my support, aware as they are of my sentiments on the Popery Bill with its concomitant and consequential evils and on the conduct of the base Apostates, who have inflicted that fatal calamity on their insulted and indignant Country.[58]

Ecumenism, as yet, had not touched the hearts in Aldingham.

Bartholomew McHugh remained as parish priest at Ulverston until his death in 1844. The chapel still stands; following its replacement by the town's present church in 1895, it became the Oddfellows' Hall and is now a furniture and antique repository. The Manor Mission continued at Ulverston under the care of the Jesuits until Fr Bernard Jarrett, S.J., handed the mission over to the care of Dr Goss, Bishop of Liverpool, in 1863, the English Catholic hierarchy having been re-established in 1850.

Notes

1. Pickering (ed.), *Statutes at Large*, 11 & 12 Guil. III cap. 4., vol. 10, pp. 315–19.
2. Ibid., 30 Car. 2, cap. 2.
3. Colin Haydon, *Anti-Catholicism in eighteenth-century England, c. 1714–80. A political and social study* (Manchester and New York: Manchester University Press, 1993) especially chapter 5.
4. Foley, *Records S.J.*, vol. 5, pp. 320–1.
5. PRO, *Forfeited Estates 1716*, p. 62.
6. Pickering (ed.), *Statutes at Large*, 1 Geo. I, Stat. 2, cap. 55, vol. 13, pp. 312–19.
7. Ibid., Geo. I, Stat. 2, cap. 50. pp. 299–30.
8. Haydon, *Anti-Catholicism*, p. 110.
9. Ibid., p. 111.
10. PRO *Forfeited Estates*, 1716, L. 2.
11. PRO Ibid., B. 62. Quoted in CRS, *Lancashire Registers*, p. 9.
12. Haydon, *Anti-Catholicism*, p. 111.
13. Foley, *Records S.J.*, vol. 7, pp. 287, 765.
14. T. G. Ward and L. Warren, *The Manor Mission of Low Furness* (Bolton: The Catholic Printing Company of Farnworth, 1979), pp. 19, 22.
15. T. G. Holt, S.J., *William Strickland and the Suppressed Jesuits*, CRS (1988), p. 7.
16. Ibid., p. 11.
17. Ibid., pp. 13–14.
18. The English Province of the Society of Jesus was divided into administrative districts, each styled a 'college'. The northern district, with headquarters at Stonyhurst was styled 'The College of St Aloysius'. For history of Stonyhurst see T. Muir, *Stonyhurst College 1593–1993* (London: James & James (Publishers) Ltd, 1992).
19. Holt, *William Strickland*, pp. 100ff.
20. B. C. Foley, 'Ann Fenwick née Benison' in *Some People of the Penal Times* (Preston: Snape & Co. 1991), pp 25–33; the Fenwick case is also referred to in Haydon, *Anti-Catholicism*, p. 174.
21. B. C. Foley, 'Robert Edward Ninth Lord Petre, Thorndon, Essex (1742–1801)', in ibid., p. 105.
22. Pickering (ed.), *Statutes at Large*, 18 Geo. III, cap. 60, vol. 32, pp. 152–4; 31 Geo. III, cap. 32, vol. 37.
23. Thomas Innes was a well-loved teacher, known to his students as 'Father Innes' at the Scottish College of Paris, and was a noted antiquarian: *A Biographical Dictionary of Emminent Scotsmen*, ed. Richard Chambers (Glasgow, Edinburgh and London: Blackie & Son, 1854), pp. 183–6.
24. T. G. Holt, 'Father West, F.S.A.', *CW2*, vol. 79 (1979), pp. 131–2.
25. West, *Antiquities of Furness*, p. 16.
26. CRS, *Lancashire Registers*, pp. 9–10.

27. Holt, 'Father West', *CW2*, vol. 79 (1979), p. 134; LRO, RCHY 3/7/26.

28. T. E. Casson, 'Diary of Edward Jackson, Vicar of Colton, for the year 1775' in *CW2*, vol. 40 (1940), p. 14. Edward Jackson was one of Fr West's correspondents, LRO, RCHY 3/7/25. This friendship with an Anglican minister at this time is in sharp contrast to the attitude of Robert Walker, vicar of Seathwaite – Wordsworth's 'Wonderful Walker' – who in the 1767 Returns stated 'We have not One Papist, or any so reputed, or even a Dissenter ... For the space of more than twenty years ... this happe [sic] unanimity has subsisted through my Chapelry'.

29. J. A. Hilton, *Catholic Lancashire From Reformation to Renewal 1559–1991* (Chichester: Phillimore, 1994), p. 82.

30. Holt, 'Father Thomas West', *CW2*, vol. 79, p. 132. LRO, RCHY 3/7/11.

31. T. Ward and L. Warren, *The Manor Mission*, p. 26; LRO, RCHY 3/7/56.

32. T. G. Holt, 'Father West, F.S.A.', *CW2*, vol. 79, p. 132; CRS, *Lancashire Registers*, p. 10.

33. Information received from Stephen Deeming, Swarthmoor Hall.

34. See below, p. 46 and endnote 40.

35. Bossy, *The English Catholic Community*, pp. 393–4; Michael Mullett, 'A Catholic Looks at Quakerism' *Quaker Studies*, vol. 2, no. 1 (Sunderland: University of Sunderland, 1997), pp. 57–64.

36. The Friends, now once again owners of Swarthmoor Hall, still extend the hand of friendship to other Christians, having recently given temporary hospitality to the Orthodox Liturgy.

37. *VCH Lancs*, vol. 8, pp. 348, 354–6; CRS, ser. 20, p. 9.

38. E. S. Worrall (ed.), *Returns of Papists 1767*, vol. 1, CRS, Occasional Papers series.

39. Ward and Warren, *The Manor Mission*, p. 23;.

40. Godfrey Anstruther, *The Seminary Priests*, p. 173; J. Gillow, *Bibliographical Dictionary of the English Catholics* (5 vols, 1885–1902), vol. 4, p. 242–3: James Lindow was born in 1729, son of James Lindow and his wife Bridget née Ormandy, both of long-established families of Ulverston. He died 5 December 1806. In his will, proved 29 January 1807, he left under £600.

41. Foley, 'Thomas West' in *Some People of the Penal Times*, pp. 81–2; LRO, RCLJ, acc. 5919/1.

42. Ward & Warren, *The Manor Mission*, p. 28.

43. Dominic A. Bellenger, *The French Exiled Clergy in the British Isles after 1789: An Historical Introduction and Working List* (Bath: Downside Abbey, 1986), p. 47. For reaction and generosity of the bishops and clergy of the Church of England, see chapter 3.

44. William Wordsworth, 'Emigrant French Clergy', *Ecclesiastical Sonnets*, in *Selected Poems of William Wordsworth* (London, New York, Toronto: Oxford University Press, 1950), p. 332.

45. Ward and Warren, *The Manor Mission*, p. 27.

46. Mr Sewell to Mr Stone, Letter 22 Feb. 1830, in *Archives of the College of St Aloysius, Rixton–Wigan Papers*, fol. 145. Archives of Society of Jesus, Mount Street, London.

47. Ibid.

48. CRS, *Lancashire Registers*, p. 11. See below for a plan of local Catholic church property. p. 56.

49. Letter, Mr Sewell to Mr Stone, *Rixton–Wigan Papers*, f. 175. Apart from these property transactions, Dr Everard used his own money to buy land 'which was totally distinct and in no way appertaining to the Mission at Ulverston'; valued at £4,000, it was sold to the Society in return for an annuity of £400 a

year for life. The list of properties makes interesting reading for Ulverston people:

Ratten Row Meadows, 5 statute acres, yearly value	40.0.0.
Barnbeck Water Meadows, 3 statute acres let for	18.0.0.
Gill Banks, 11a. 1r. 16p. let for	39.0.0.
Church Meadow, 1 acre and half statute, let for	9.0.0.
A little field adjoining to Church Meadow	8.0.0.
A Garden at Gill Banks, let for	0.15.0.
A Garden behind the House and Chapel let for	0.15.0.
A Stable at Ratten Row, let for	1.0.0.
	£116.10.0.

N.B. Taxes and other expenses reduce the amount to about £100.

Mr Sewell realised that a return of only £100 set against an annuity of £400 was not, actuarially, a good investment for the Society, and contingencies were made for Dr Everard's living longer than calculated or expected.

50. Playing cards for money, seems to have been an accepted entertainment for gentlemen, even of the cloth. Edward Jackson records in his diary, the gains and losses he sustained at cards over the twelvemonths of 1775. His greatest loss was on 28 November when he lost 7s. 0d.: Casson, 'Diary of Edward Jackson', *CW2*, vol. 40, pp. 27–45.

51. Ward and Warren, *The Manor Mission*, pp. 29–30.

52. Ibid., pp. 30–31.

53. CRS, *Lancashire Registers*, p. 11.

54. Dr Everard to Mr Stone, Letter 7 Sept. 1816, *Rixton–Wigan Papers*, f. 81.

55. Mr Sewell to Mr Stone, Letter 1818, *Rixton–Wigan Papers*. f. 141.

56. Mr Sewell to Mr Stone, Letter 22 Feb. 1830, *Rixton–Wigan Papers*, f. 145.

57. Letter to the Bishop of Chester, CRO Barrow ZS 1170. This material is also reproduced in David Borwick, *An English Provincial Society, North Lancashire 1770–1820*, Unpublished Ph.D. Thesis, University of Lancaster, 1994, pp. 339–40.

58. Open letter to John Wilson Patten from the Rev. John Stonard, printed by S. Tyson, Ulverston (5 Jan. 1830), CRO Barrow BPR/21 I37/1. Also reproduced in Borwick, *English Provincial Society*, p. 340. For further reading concerning the Catholic Emancipation Act, see Gilley and Shiels, *A History of Religion*, chapters 14 and 15. For the reaction of the *literati* both before and after the passing of the act, see Kevin L. Morris, 'Rescuing The Scarlet Woman: The Promotion of Catholicism in English Literature, 1829–1850', *Recusant History*, vol. 22, no. 1 (1994).

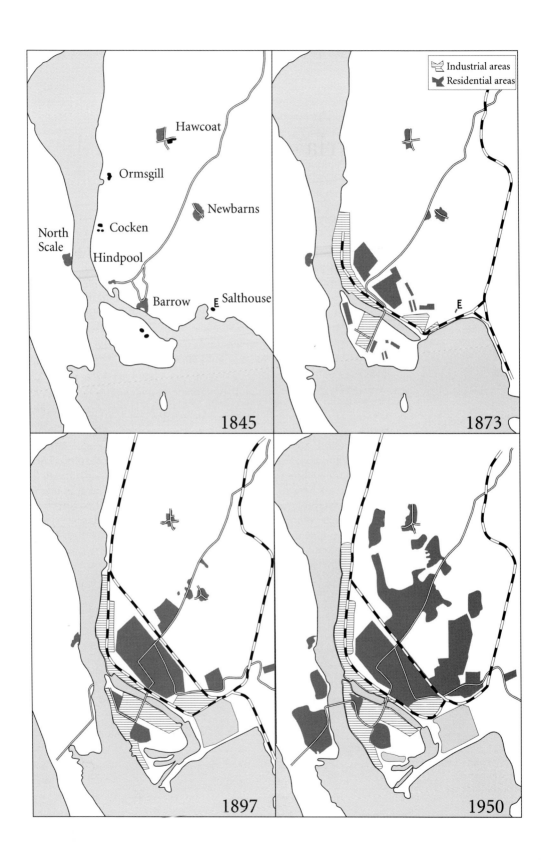

Hawcoat

Ormsgill

Newbarns

North
Scale

Cocken

Hindpool

Barrow

E Salthouse

1845

Industrial areas
Residential areas

E

1873

1897

1950

CHAPTER SIX

The nineteenth century – industrialisation and re-birth

In the nineteenth-century Furness experienced the greatest social and economic change in its history, and before we return to our account of the development of the peninsula's Catholic history, we need to fill in some details of the industrialisation of the south-western tip of the region, shifting the centre of gravity and transforming the composition of its Catholic community beyond recognition. For it was Barrow that became the regional centre of the unfolding Industrial Revolution, as it was to become the dynamo of Furness's vibrant Catholic renaissance. In Edward Baines' History and Gazetteer of the County Palatine of Lancashire, first published in 1824, Barrow is referred to 'as a small hamlet a few miles west of Dalton on the sea coast'. In fact, one might say it was hardly on the map. Furness Abbey had had a grange at the 'hamelete of Barrayhede' (which assumed the form of Barrow in the nineteenth century), valued in the sixteenth century at £11 per annum. The grange at Byggar (or Biggar) – was obviously of greater importance, being valued at £14 12s. 0d.[1] Subsequent indications show that Walney Island, which included the granges of Byggar, North Scale, Southend and Northend, had a higher valuation, and figured in the history of the area more prominently, than 'Barrayhede'. The grange established by the monks on the site of Barrow consisted of eight homesteads, but soon after the surrender of the Abbey two were pulled down and rebuilt at Hindpool. Over the centuries, these original homesteads disappeared, some being rebuilt on the same sites, but prior to 1780 Barrow consisted of only five farm-houses, two cottages and the 'Ship Inn' built right on the foreshore, barely out of reach of the spring tides – eight dwellings in all.[2]

The monks had found that the Furness peninsula was rich in high-grade haematite ore deposits which they mined and smelted. By the early seventeenth century many small bloomeries were in existence in Low Furness; these, after a systematic process of amalgamation, formed themselves by 1736 into two fairly sizeable companies: the Newland Iron Company and the Backbarrow Iron Company. Both had built furnaces, superseding the bloomeries, but still relied on charcoal for fuel.[3] From 1745 the Backbarrow Iron Company began exporting iron ore in small amounts from Barrow. By 1782 the Newland Iron Company made Barrow its principal port, and iron-ore yards and jetties were built to accommodate this traffic. Although Piel had a natural harbour and the deeper water, Barrow had the advantage of having two islands protecting its shore: the small island which lies to the west and close to the Barrow shore, which originally was known as Old Barrow Island, but which, on incorporation of the borough in June 1867

MAP 2 (*opposite*). Growth of Barrow-in-Furness. Based on F. Barnes, *Barrow and District*, by courtesy of Barrow Borough council and Ron Smith.

and the division of the town into wards, became Barrow Island; and the larger and longer island of Walney which faces the Irish Sea and protects both Barrow Island and Barrow from storms.

The two iron-mining companies mentioned constituted the trickle that was to become the flood which, during the Industrial Revolution, would overwhelm the tiny village of Barrow. By 1801 the number of dwelling houses had risen to eleven, only three more than in 1780. Twenty-one years later there was a slight increase, there being now a resident blacksmith, a butcher, a shoe-maker and a maltster.[4] In 1829 there were sixteen dwellings, but only two on Barrow Island. We do not know the number of children in the district, though there was a school; some time prior to 1835 two master mariners came to live in Barrow and also Thomas Hodgson, the Customs Officer, the only inhabitant who was a Catholic.[5] By 1843 the number of dwelling houses had risen to twenty-eight, possibly housing a population of about 150–160. It is important to bear in mind these population estimates to appreciate what happened in the following twenty years, in which Barrow's mineral and industrial potential was to be fully exploited and spearheaded by the two men who owned the mineral rights of the area and who were to be responsible for the coming of the railway in June 1846:[6] the Duke of Buccleuch, and William Cavendish, Earl of Burlington, later to become seventh Duke of Devonshire. It was to St Mary of Furness that the new Furness Railway looked when forming its logo; the Company adopted the great seal of Furness Abbey, with St Mary in the centre.[7]

Meanwhile, Henry Schneider, a cousin of the Schneider who gave his name to the Schneider Cup, together with his brother John, both of whom were members of a world-wide mining company, began a geological exploration of Furness for iron ore. After finding rich deposits in the area in 1851 Schneider joined with Robert Hanney, the Scottish iron-master, in 1857. Schneider, Hanney and Company started mining and exporting ore and then built the Barrow Iron Works in 1859 to supply the demand for the much sought-after haematite pig-iron.[8] The Furness Railway, providing transport of the ore from the mines to the Iron Works at Hindpool, Barrow, and from there to the jetties, was to prove to be of great economic benefit to Barrow. But the railway was to bring to the town another asset: James Ramsden, a young man of twenty-three years, who was appointed to the post of superintendent of the Furness Railway Company in 1846, and who remained with the Company until his retirement in 1895.[9] Ramsden, knighted in 1872 was, with Schneider, one of the two outstanding founding fathers of Barrow. Ramsden was far-seeing: in 1856 the Bessemer process of making steel was invented, but it needed high quality pig-iron to be successful, and this was exactly what Schneider and Hanney were producing. Ramsden formed his own company in 1864 to manufacture steel, but on 1 January 1866 the Barrow Iron Works of Schneider, Hanney and Company, together with the ore mines they owned, were amalgamated with James Ramsden's firm, and the Barrow Haematite Steel Company came into existence, supplying steel rails for the expanding railways throughout the world.[10]

Emerging as the new focus of Furness Catholicism, Barrow now began to grow at an amazing rate, though its links with the ancient Abbey were noted carefully, as in a report in *Soulbey's Ulverston Advertiser* of 1863 suggesting a comparison between Victorian industrial enterprise and the 'industry and skill' of the monks, evicted by the 'confounded scamp' Henry VIII:

> Barrow has a history to make: and when Barrow has such a history as this abbey, glorious even in ruins, many and many a generation of iron-masters must have passed away. Don't talk to us of the badness of the monks; they were our forefathers, sir, soothed the last moments of many an English man and English woman and taught many a child the way to heaven ... But the national character of Old England was laid ... in a not unimportant degree by these very monks – call them foolish, stupid, or what you may. Beautiful, we say, even in ruins, venerable even in decay, the old ivy-grown stones were once the church of our fore-fathers. Many a brave Englishman worshipped there in the old storied days. And was it not in those days that we won Agincourt, and wrung the Great Charter from John? We thought so as we roamed the ruins of Furness Abbey.[11]

FIGURE 13 (*left*). Paint Shop in Newland Street, Barrow, first Mass centre in Barrow.

FIGURE 14. Fr Bilsborrow, first parish priest at St Mary of Furness, Barrow; subsequently Bishop of Salford.

The building of the blast furnaces and the Bessemer steel convertors was concurrent with the development of Barrow as a port. The development of the docks, was, by far, the most important cause of Barrow's expansion. The second Barrow Harbour Act of 1863 empowered the Furness Railway to deepen and enlarge the natural channel between Barrow Island and the mainland. When W. E. Gladstone opened Devonshire dock in September

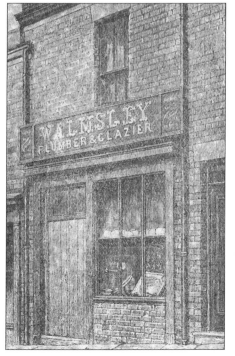

1867, he said that he envisaged Barrow as 'a rival to Liverpool' – his birthplace. Buccleuch Dock followed in February 1873 and Ramsden Dock in March 1879.[12] This meant, of course, that labour was needed, for both the construction of the iron and steel works, but also, and on a much larger scale, for the excavation and building of the docks. Almost all of this work-force had to come from outside, and much of it from Ireland whence the potato famine of 1846 drove a whole peasantry – almost all of them Catholics, it goes without saying – out in search of food and work. By 1866, in the space of twenty-three years, the population of Barrow had risen literally one hundred-fold to 16,000, an incredible growth. We can only estimate the probable percentage of this 16,000 who were Irish Catholics; but by comparing the figures available for Cardiff and Manchester it is likely that the percentage would be at least twenty-five per cent – 4,000.[13]

This sudden and huge expansion in the Catholic population and the rapidly industrialising town was a challenge requiring a ready response from the Church within Furness, still, at this juncture, based on Ulverston, where, presumably, Barrow's overwhelmingly Irish population of Catholics walked to Mass on Sunday mornings until the provision first of a priest, and finally a church in the town in the 1860s. That response can be said to have formed a local reflection of what Cardinal Newman called a 'Second Spring', the extraordinary Victorian renaissance of English Catholicism from what was, in some areas, a near extinction in the eighteenth century and its radical re-alignment away from its post-Reformation rural orientation towards Britain's new urban and industrial centres of gravity. In our account of nineteenth-century developments our focus will be primarily the rise of renascent Catholicism in industrial Barrow and its parishes, though we shall take account of developments in Ulverston, Dalton and elsewhere. Barrow was indeed the epitome of the new Irish-oriented Catholicism that arose in Victorian Britain: in London, the Midlands, the North-East, South-Wales, South-West Lancashire and South-West Scotland.[14] At the same time, this new industrial-orientated, large and largely proletarian Catholic community, whose members played a vital part in Britain's economic and industrial mastery could hardly be overlooked in the development of the country's Christian life. Indeed, a marked feature of our narration in these final chapters is the gradual emergence, at first extremely tentative, of an ecumenical spirit.

By 1858 Fr Bernard Jarrett, S.J., then in charge of the Ulverston Mission, the direct successor to the Manor Mission, was travelling to Barrow to celebrate Mass in the house of Joseph Walmsley who lived, first at 57, Greengate Street, next in the Strand, and finally in a house on the corner of Newland Street and Hindpool Road. When the Jesuits handed over the Ulverston Mission to Dr Goss, the second Bishop of Liverpool, Fr Peter Laverty was given charge of the mission, the only one in Lancashire North of the Sands. This was in 1863, by which time the population explosion in Barrow was well under way and Fr Laverty was having to travel the nine miles to Barrow, very often during the night, to administer the Last Sacraments, as well as travelling the same distance to celebrate Mass at Mr Walmsley's house. Bishop Goss was anxious that Barrow, along with Con-

iston, also then a mining centre, should have its own church and pressed
Fr Laverty to preach from Carlisle to Lancaster to raise funds, and to make
approaches to obtain a site.[15]

By June 1864, through the good offices of James Ramsden, the Duke of
Devonshire's steward in Barrow, the Duke offered a piece of land 'for the
Roman Catholics of this town and district for the erection, on the Hindpool
estate, of a place of worship capable of accommodating from 600 to 700
persons, together with a school-house and residence for the officiating
priests. An eminent architect is now preparing the plans.'[16] The 'eminent
architect' was in fact Edward Welby Pugin, and the church he designed, St
Mary of Furness, is considered to be the finest example of his work in the
north of England. The style was 'Pugin Gothic', copied from his more
famous father Augustus. By 1865 Bishop Goss realised that a resident priest
would have to be sent to Barrow to found a mission in its own right,
choosing Fr John Bilsborrow, ordained on February 16th 1865 and in early
March taking responsibility for the new parish of St Mary's. Joseph Walmsley gave him the use of his paint shop in Newland Street, which he used,
pending the building of St Mary's, as chapel and school, while he lived in
a nearby cottage. Fr Bilsborrow was advised by Bishop Goss 'to have courage
and let down his net in the name of the Lord, and have a good hope that
in a short time we shall see the mission of Barrow placed solid on a lasting
foundation, and the neighbourhood of Furness once more, as in olden days,
the garden of the Lord'.[17] John Bilsborrow certainly did 'let down his net',
for on 8 July 1866, the foundation stone of the new church was laid by Dr
Goss. *The Barrow Herald and Advertiser* gave a full report of the ceremony,
in minute detail, with a translation of the Latin text, together with a verbatim
account of the bishop's sermon. Although the cold, wet and windy weather
was far from favourable, a large crowd of upwards of 2,000 assembled to
witness the proceedings. Bishop Goss's sermon resembled the local news-
paper report of 1863 in recalling the lost glories of the ancient Abbey, now
on the doorstep of industrial Barrow:

> Could I only take you back to that year in 1127, in this very month of
> July – nay within two days of the very day of which we are now met –
> to the Valley of the Deadly Nightshade – you would see there the
> venerable Abbey of Furness first beginning to rise from the ground; for
> it was on that day that Stephen, Earl of Moreton, afterwards king of
> England laid the foundation stone of Furness Abbey in the immediate
> neighbourhood of this place. In those days it was the shelter of the
> oppressed, of the weary, of the poor and it was there that the man who
> had been pursued by the minions of the law found shelter until he could
> be tried by a jury ...

However, the bishop was quick to reassure his audience that Victorian
Catholics had no designs on former monastic property, or, by extension,
on the status quo in Victorian England. Indeed he paid a gracious implied
tribute to the duke, the then owner of the estate who had, of course,
provided the site for the new church:

... the monasteries have been swept away; we care not to restore them; we do not want to take them back; we believe they have fallen into generous hands, and into the possession of liberal men, who with a noble generosity manage the property which descended from the monks of old.[18]

In August 1867 the church was ready for worship, the entire cost being between £5,000 and £6,000.[19] One might compare the cost of this building with that of St Peter's church (now cathedral) at Lancaster, which cost £15,000 and the land £2,200.[20]

The solemn opening took place on Wednesday 28 August 1867. The building was not complete, for the tower and spire which were part of Pugin's plans had still to be added. Bishop Goss presided over the ceremony, and High Mass was celebrated in his presence. No doubt conscious of the fact, that as at the laying of the foundation-stone, there were many non-Catholics in the congregation, the bishop, in his sermon, defended Catholic beliefs. He took the opportunity to stress the fact that, although the Church set up images of saints, as was the case in this building, 'they did not pray to them, for there could be no efficacy in the wood or stone, but they were set up to remind them of the holiness of the exercise and to lead their thoughts to God'. After the close of the service, about a hundred of the clergy and their friends sat down to dinner at the Harbour Hotel.[21] The following Sunday the services in connection with the opening were continued with High Mass at 10.30 a.m., followed by a sermon by the Rev. Canon George Gillow, of Preston. Like Dr Goss's on the previous Wednesday, Canon Gillow's was didactic and perhaps a little defensive, vindicating the doctrines of the Catholic Church, especially transubstantiation. These sermons were reported verbatim in the local press, and both Canon Gillow and the Bishop of Liverpool took advantage of the press coverage to explain the doctrines of the Church. Canon Gillow concluded his sermon with an earnest appeal for the support of their church in this town. The collections during the day amounted to £46.[22]

The Catholics were, of course, not the only ones to be building churches at this time, for the influx of new inhabitants meant that all denominations needed places of worship, though when the *Barrow Herald* in its issue of 23 October 1871 counted the town's new churches – Church of England, Church of Scotland and Methodist – it had to admit that 'the largest body of Christians are those connected with the Latin Church and as Macaulay was unable to conceive the possibility of that community ever ceasing to be what it has been, we, as journalists are in duty bound to record the position which it has attained in Barrow'; record it they did, in a report that showed the intense fervour and dedication of the Catholic community in Barrow.[23]

With the rising population, the need for schools also became acute: funds continued to be raised by means of 'charity sermons' (sermons preached by a visiting priest, admittance to which was by the purchase of a ticket), the most popular means of raising money for the Church in that period, but in February 1869 the parish suffered a severe blow by the serious illness of Fr Bilsborrow who was struck down with fever contracted while ministering to his flock (probably small-pox or typhoid, both of which were raging in Barrow at that time): he recovered, though, and spent his convalescence visiting friends throughout the diocese, seeking financial assistance for the mission.[24] In May 1871 Fr Bilsborrow was back with his flock, urging the congregation to be generous at the collections at charity sermons which were preached by Canon Gillow and by Dean Walker of Lancaster in order to raise money for the education of the children of Barrow's rapidly increasing Catholic population.[25] Aided by generous donations from the Duke of Devonshire and Alderman Schneider, Barrow's Catholics were able, by October 1871, to invite the mayor, James Ramsden, to lay the foundation stone for the Catholic schools, which were completed and opened in August of the following year.

Fr Bilsborrow's health had been giving concern for some time, and after seeing his efforts to establish a school crowned with success, he was content when Bishop Goss decided to move him to a country mission at Newsham (now re-named Newhouse) near Preston: after establishing a new mission at Catforth, he returned in August 1882 to Lancashire North of the Sands, to a mission at the new resort of Grange-over-Sands, where Fr Massey of Ulverston had purchased land. For eighteen months Mass was celebrated in Kent's Ford House, the residence of John Sutcliffe-Witham Esq ... Fr Bilsborrow saw the foundation-stone of Grange's new church, dedicated to St Charles, laid on 29 May 1883. After teaching moral theology at the diocesan seminary in Upholland, Fr Bilsborrow was consecrated Bishop of Salford in 1892 and remained there until his death in 1903.[26] He was a priest whose apostolic zeal drove him, ill health notwithstanding, to build three churches, two of which were in Furness.

Following Fr Bilsborrow's move to the Preston area, Fr James Parkinson was sent as rector of the Barrow mission in 1872. Fr Parkinson made the education of children his priority, while the parishioners found the money to build a presbytery in 1874, followed by the consecration of the Catholic part of the new town cemetery.[27] The installation of a new pulpit during Fr Parkinson's ministry was followed during the tenure of his successor, Fr William Gordon, by the installation in February 1876 of a new altar in keeping with the architecture of the church, costing £260 and still standing today. The altar's Caen stone pinnacle surmounts the tabernacle; carved stone work represents the figures of Our Lord and Our Lady, SS. Peter, Paul, James and John, with representations of the Last Supper and the Adoration of the Lamb flanking the tabernacle. Consecrating the altar, Bishop O'Reilly, the successor to Dr Goss, who had died in 1872, recalled in his sermon that it was only eleven years since the first priest had been appointed to Barrow, before which Catholics had been an almost unknown body. Fr Bilsborrow, who was making a return visit, preached at the evening service and reminded the congregation of his first Mass at Barrow in the small room over Mr Walmsley's paint shop on 11 March 1865 when 'the tears of the dumb people were shed when they saw a priest amongst them'.[28] On a more practical level and reflecting the Victorians' twin love of technology and desire for comfort, 'a heating apparatus, after the most approved patents' was installed later, in November 1876, at a cost of £140. Bishop O'Reilly returned in the same year to confirm over eighty parishioners [29] and in 1877, with a donation from the Furness Railway Company, Fr Gordon provided a mixed school for Catholic children on Barrow Island,[30] forming the nucleus of what was to become St Patrick's parish.

The Barrow Catholic community felt itself very much part of the universal Church, and marked the death of Pope Pius IX in 1878 with deep mourning in a series of services in which the late pontiff's achievements, including the convening of the First Vatican Council and proclamation of papal infallibility, the definition of the dogma of the Immaculate Conception and the restoration of the hierarchy to England and Wales were honoured.[31]

The expansion of Barrovian Catholicism had a dynamising effect on the regeneration of the Church in the Furness peninsula, and certainly in the south-western extremity. Indeed, work continued on the provision for worship in Barrow's immediate vicinity, with a temporary chapel opened by Fr Gordon in Dalton in 1878. In opening the temporary building, Fr Gordon recalled both the earlier revival of Barrow Catholicism when some of the congregation would be among those who had 'knelt in the rain outside Walmsley's paint shop without thought of the effect on their Sunday clothes and thought nothing of walking four, nay seven miles to Barrow from Dalton and Ireleth', and also the earlier history of recusancy followed by emancipation.[32] Fr Gordon began the building of a school-chapel and presbytery at Dalton; these were completed by his successor, Fr Caffrey, in November 1879; the chapel, dedicated to Our Lady of the Rosary, was designed to accommodate some 200 persons.[33]

On 13 September 1879 Fr Gordon preached his farewell sermon. Though what we know as ecumenism was hardly known in those embattled days, Fr Gordon showed intimations of better understanding between Christian denominations in recalling the generosity his Church had received from those outside it, especially Sir James Ramsden (as he now was), and Mr Schneider.[34] During his period at St Mary's, the choir had also achieved a considerable reputation in the town and local press, and their choice of music for a Mass at which Fr Bilsborrow preached a charity sermon, though eclectic, showed that they were prepared to be challenged; it also reflected the rather 'secular' nature of the Church's music in this period before the full official re-adoption of 'Gregorian' forms by Pius X in his motu proprio of 1903. They sang the *Kyrie* from Weber's Mass in G; a *Gloria* by Farmer; at the Offertory the first part of Zingarelli's *Laudate*; the *Credo* from Haydn's No. 13 Mass; the *Benedictus* and *Agnus Dei* from Haydn's Mass No. 9, and at the end of Mass the final part of the *Laudate*.[35] Christmas Day 1880 saw St Mary's choir excelling themselves with a rendering of Haydn's No. 3 Mass, the 'Imperial': this brought a glowing report in the local press, which commented that 'this is one of the finest masses of this famous composer and perhaps one of the most difficult. The way it was rendered deserves no small amount of praise'.[36]

Fr Edmund Caffrey, the next priest appointed to St Mary's, was to remain there for the rest of the century, spending his time building up the parish

FIGURE 15.
Fr Edward Caffrey.

and extending the schools. In taking charge of the mission, he also inherited a debt of £2,000 which he promptly addressed himself to clearing. By 1881, though, it had become obvious that more school accommodation was needed and in February of that year Fr Caffrey announced plans for additional schools,[37] including a separate school for 280 girls, which were completed that year. That same year saw an organ installed in the gallery at a cost of £500, and in 1882 Stations of the Cross were donated, followed by carving on the capitals, and handsome new altar rails carved in walnut and teak depicting the Twelve Apostles, and on the gates *Ecce Homo* and *Mater Dolorosa*.[38]

Trouble in Ireland over the Land Act of 1881 resulted in the assassination in Phoenix Park, Dublin, of Lord Frederick Cavendish in May 1882. With the local connections that Barrow had with the Cavendish family, who were the principal architects of its rise, the town was immediately in a state of mourning and horror. Protest meetings against the Fenians were held all over Barrow. On the day of his funeral all the shops and works in Barrow closed down in sympathy and tribute, while all the churches in the town held services. St Mary's, whose very location was the product of Cavendish generosity, was suitably decorated in mourning for its service; on the front of the altar was a black antipendium, in the centre of which was a white cross and a wreath. The pulpit was covered with crêpe and as a mark of signal respect to the Cavendish family which had so generously endowed the Catholic community, a catafalque used four years earlier to mark the obsequies of Pius IX, was once more brought into service. Fr Duffy, the curate, led the service, the *De Profundis* was recited, followed by the choir singing the *Miserere*, after which the usual prayers for the dead were recited. The hymn 'Days and moments quickly flying' was sung by the choir. Fr Duffy preached, denouncing the horrible crime and expressing sympathy to the ducal House of Devonshire. The service concluded with the dead March in Saul.[39]

The early nineteenth century had seen the Catholic Emancipation Act of 1829 which gave, amongst other freedoms, the right to build churches with spires and towers. This freedom, together with the population explosion caused through the development of the mineral potential in the area and the building of the railway and the creation of the docks, meant that the Catholic population of Barrow had increased beyond recognition and the second half of the century was marked by the expansion of Catholic worship in the area; the most notable example being the building of the church of St Mary of Furness. This marked the shift of the Catholic centre of Furness from Ulverston, where, in the eighteenth and early nineteenth centuries, the Manor Mission had kept the faith alive, to Barrow.

The initial responsibility of making the Barrow mission viable had rested on Fr Laverty at Ulverston. The Bishop had realised the developing importance of Barrow, and also of the needs of the small Lake-district Catholic community at Coniston. In September 1864 he had instructed his secretary to write to Fr Laverty at Ulverston:

> The Bishop is most anxious about Barrow and Coniston ... he has brought Barrow to the notice of every congregation ... he is anxious to know what you are doing ... He hopes you are trying to get land at Coniston ...

Fr Laverty acquired the necessary land at Coniston where the Sacred Heart Church was built in 1872. The Bishop, Dr Goss, did not give Fr Laverty an easy time: for example on 9 January 1865 he wrote to him, 'I am surprised to find that out of a population of 200 you only have thirty at catechism on Sundays'. On 12 April 1865 Fr Laverty got another episcopal broadside: '... I hope your people are coming well up to their duties – they need great improvement on the score of attending Mass for I find in one Sunday only 162 present, while in another there are 309, a greater difference than an inclemency of weather can account for.'[40]

Fr Laverty began to feel the strain of extending the original Manor Mission, retired from Ulverston in poor health in 1877 and was succeeded by Fr William Massey. Fr Massey's first task was to address what he considered was an urgent necessity, the improvement of the existing school premises in Back Lane, behind the church, which were housed in some small cottages. He raised the standard of the teaching, both secular and religious, but realised that new schools were the only ultimate solution. He secured a central site in Ulverston with sufficient land to build church, school and presbytery. The school was the priority, and his principal desire was to see this task completed. It was not to be, though the school building project was well under way when his health failed, he was obliged to resign the Manor Mission towards the end of 1886. However, he recovered and resumed his priestly duties until January 1887 when Fr Thomas. B. Allan was appointed.[41]

Though Catholicism in the older market town of Ulverston underwent an appreciable expansion during this period, it was the expansion of the Church in Barrow that reveals it as a regional archetype of the new, Irish-immigrant, industrial Catholicism of the nineteenth century. It is noteworthy also that, in a Victorian, and enthusiastically Protestant, England in which suspicions of 'popery' were latent and were indeed re-awakened by such acts of 'papal aggression' as the restoration of the hierarchy in 1850, powerful and wealthy interests in the Barrow area – Buccleuch, Devonshire, Ramsden, Schneider, and the Furness Railway Company, – as well as the influential local press, were cordial towards the Catholic community, in terms of material generosity and of sympathetic reporting. Such positive attitudes pointed the way towards the early dawnings of ecumenical attitudes which we shall explore in the next chapters.

Notes

1. PRO, *Valor Ecclesiaticus – Hen. VIII.* vol. v p. 269.
2. W. B. Kendall and H. Gaythorpe 'The Village of Barrow – owners and occupiers in 1843', *Annual Reports, Proceedings etc. of Barrow Field Naturalist Field Club, and Literary and Scientific Association.* vol. 17, pp. 181–91 (1909).
3. Barnes, *Barrow and District*, pp. 74–8.
4. Kendal and Gaythorpe 'The Village of Barrow', p. 185.
5. BRL, *Centenary Celebrations: The Church of St Mary of Furness, Barrow-in-Furness. 1865–1965* (Desktop publication, no pagination, 1965). LC 200 FE/CHU.
6. David Joy, *A Regional History of the Railways of Great Britain: Railways of the Lake Counties* (Melksham, Wilts: David St John Thomas, 1990), vol. 14, pp. 97–8.
7. *The Barrow Herald* incorporated this same seal into their masthead from the first issue of their broadsheet in 1863; in 1865 the Furness and South Cumberland Building Society, now the Furness Building Society, also took the seal of St Mary of Furness as their 'house style'.
8. Barnes, *Barrow and District*, p. 96.
9. Ibid., p. 89.
10. Ibid., p. 96.
11. *Soulbey's Ulverston Advertiser and General Intelligencer*, 8 Oct. 1863.
12. Barnes, *Barrow and District*, p. 91.
13. Irish Catholics formed about one third (10,000) of Cardiff's 1861 population of 32,954: John Hickey, *Urban Catholics, in England and Wales from 1829 to the Present Day* (London, Dublin and Melbourne: Geoffrey Chapman, 1967), pp. 58, 62.
14. Edward Norman, *The English Catholic Church in the Nineteenth Century* (Oxford: Clarendon Press, 1984); James Derek Holmes, *More Roman Than Rome: English Catholicism in the Nineteenth Century* (London: Burns and Oates, 1978).
15. Ward and Warren, *The Manor Mission of Low Furness*, pp. 38–9.

16. *Barrow Herald and Advertiser*, 25 June 1864.

17. Ibid., 24 June 1865.

18. Ibid., 14 July 1866.

19. *Centenary Celebrations.*

20. Richard Newman Billington and John Brownhill, *St Peters, Lancaster* (London and Edinburgh: Sands & Co., 1910), p. 106.

21. *Barrow Herald*, 23 Aug. 1867.

22. Ibid., 7 Sept. 1867.

23. Ibid., 23 Oct. 1871; The journalist was referring to Macaulay's observation in (*Essays, 1843, Edinburgh Review*, vol. 3): The Roman Church may still exist in undiminished vigour when some traveller from New Zealand shall, in the midst of a vast solitude, take his stand on a broken arch of London Bridge to sketch the ruins of St Paul's. For full report see Appendix 2.

24. *Centenary Celebrations.*

25. *Barrow Herald*, 13 May 1871.

26. *Catholic Family Annual and Almanac for the Dioceses of Liverpool and Shrewsbury*, 1899 (Liverpool: The Catholic Printing Company, 1899).

27. *Barrow Herald*, 9 May 1874.

28. Ibid., 2 Feb. 1876.

29. Ibid., 25 Nov. 1876.

30. *Centenary Celebrations.*

31. *Barrow Herald*, 23 Feb. 1876.

32. Ibid., 22 Oct. 1878.

33. Edmund Caffrey, *Catholicity in Barrow* (BRL, LC 200 FE/MAR), pp. 130–1.

34. *Barrow Herald*, 16 Sept. 1879.

35. Ibid., 23 Nov. 1878.

36. Ibid., 4 Jan. 1881.

37. Ibid., 8 Feb. 1881.

38. Ibid., 25 Nov. 1882.

39. Ibid., 13 May 1882.

40. Ward and Warren, *The Manor Mission of Low Furness*, pp. 39–40, letters are at LRO, RcUl.

41. Ibid., pp. 41–2.

CHAPTER SEVEN

Controversy and the birth of Ecumenism

Events in the 1880s exposed some of the central dilemmas of Barrovian Catholicism. The steady erosion of indigenous Catholicism in the Furness Peninsula, in contrast with the situation elsewhere in Lancashire where a native recusancy had survived, ensured that the area's Catholic revival took place – as it did in other parts of Britain such as South Wales, where home-grown Catholicism had all-but expired – under Irish immigrant auspices, linked to the rise of heavy industry and the importation of its work-force. It might have been expected that the Hibernisation of Catholicism in south-western Furness would have presented a conflict of allegiance when the Irish Fenians struck down a scion of the Cavendish family who had done much to promote Barrow Catholicism.

However, this was not the case. The news of the assassination of Lord Frederick Cavendish on Saturday 6 May 1882, in Phoenix Park, Dublin, reached Barrow the following day. The news was received first with stunned disbelief, then profound shock and horror by all its citizens. Meetings were held at all the main places of employment to register sorrow and to send messages of sympathy to the Cavendish family. The workers at the Barrow Hematite Steel Company in particular felt it as almost a family loss, since Lord Frederick had been one of the directors of the firm. On Monday 8 May all the day-shift met at 5.30 p.m. and proposed an expression of sorrow, as reported in *The Barrow Herald*, 'for the dastardly and atrocious murder of Her Majesty's principal Secretary of State for Ireland while honestly performing his duties, and of deep sympathy with Lady Cavendish [Lord Frederick's widow] and his Grace the Duke of Devonshire'. After passing the resolution, the Press reports, 'the meeting dispersed in mournful silence'. On the same evening the employees of the Barrow Shipbuilding Company also met to pass a number of resolutions, 'expressing deep and heartfelt sympathy to that good old nobleman, the Duke of Devonshire and to Lady Cavendish and all the Cavendish family in their sad bereavement'. 'No person,' the proposer said, 'would lay the assassination at the door of any right-minded Irishman, and no right-minded Irishman would have a word to say in defence.' The whole tenor of the resolutions was one of sorrow and utter abhorrence. The final resolution was 'that a record of the resolutions should be sent to Sir James Ramsden with a request that they be forwarded to his Grace the Duke of Devonshire and Lady Cavendish'. The local press were particularly impressed with the atmosphere of this meeting. They reported that 'during the speeches no revengeful thought [against the Fenians] was breathed. Complete silence accompanied the solemn, unanimous raising of hands to each resolution put to the meeting. Not a word of anger or ill-feeling disturbed the quiet and somewhat sad deportment of the assembly'. Given the numbers of Irish and Irish-descended in the workforce of the Barrow Shipbuilding Company, many of those present at this protest movement would have been Irish-Catholic.

Meetings of all the clubs and societies in the town were called, but two in particular are worthy of mention to indicate the relationship between the town and the Catholic community, which, as a result of patterns of migrations examined in Chapter 6, was mostly Irish. One was of the clergy and ministers in the town, called at the invitation of Sir James Ramsden, and held at the General Offices of the Furness Railway Company on the night of Tuesday 9 May; the clergy of the Church of England and the Free Churches were at this gathering, and a telegram was received from Fr Caffrey expressing his inability to attend but his readiness to fall in with any arrangements and resolutions that might be made at the meeting. The other meeting, held on the same evening, was that of the members of St Mary's Catholic Club, held in their club room over St Mary's School. Fr Duffy took the chair and reported that he had received a telegram from Fr Caffrey, who was in Liverpool, asking him to call a meeting to express local Catholics' outrage at the assassination. He was sure that all Catholics of Barrow, especially Irish Catholics 'on whose soil the foul deed had been committed, would sincerely deplore it'. The seconder, Mr J. Bains, said that 'no doubt, logically, the people of England would attach a certain amount of blame to Ireland and Irishmen, whereas ... every man ... in Ireland – excepting a small handful who were the instigators and abetters of this crime – would deplore it as much as anyone in Barrow'. The meeting felt that it was right that Catholics should grieve, for the generosity of the Cavendish family to the Catholics had been great.[1] As we have described in the previous chapter, St Mary's marked the funeral of Lord Frederick Cavendish with a fitting service of respect.

Thus this harrowing deed did not divide the town along Catholic – Protestant or Irish – English lines but rather drew it together in a shared grief, – even though instances of divisions between Irish and English loyalty will occur in the pages that follow. The doctrinal differences between the denominations remained of course, strongly etched. As on Merseyside and Clydeside, Ireland's own divisions between Catholic and 'Orange' Protestantism were imported into the area: in October 1883, a Mr Devlyn, an Irish Protestant agitator gave public lectures in one of the town's theatres attacking the Catholic Church. He was so provocative in his diatribes that one woman, presumably Catholic, verbally assaulted him in the street. This attracted a crowd of 'six or seven Irish roughs' and a public disturbance ensued. The police were called and arrests were made, but the outcome, when the rioters appeared before the magistrates, was that they were all fined one pound each, but Devlin was told by the mayor, not to continue his lectures, and warned that if he did he would be bound over.[2] The civic authorities were proud that their town was free from religious acrimony and made sure that this kind of incident should not recur.

In 1884 Fr Caffrey cut the first sod for a new school-chapel on Barrow

Island, dedicated, in view of the fact that the Catholic community in Barrow was now predominately Irish, to St Patrick. This chapel, built at a cost of £2,000,[3] was served from St Mary's, with one Mass on a Sunday morning at 9.30, and on Thursdays and Holydays at 8.30 a.m.[4] In the following year St Mary's required a new sacristy, and the presbytery was extended, all at a cost of £850. Nine stained glass windows were placed in the sanctuary apse at a cost of £100: Our Lady, St Joseph, and St John; three English saints: St Edward the Confessor, St Begh,[5] and St Thomas of Canterbury; three Irish: St. Patrick St Brigid and St Columba. In 1886 extensions were made to the boys' school, and land was bought for a convent in Nelson Street at a cost of £1,200, in the hope of attracting a community of nuns to Barrow.[6]

Christmas Day 1885 saw the unveiling of a new memorial window, the gift of Mr Reuben O'Neill Pearson,[7] a solicitor in Ulverston, in memory of his mother, Mrs. Ann Pearson, who had died on Christmas day the previous year. The window is a representation of St Ann and St Elizabeth, with the Agony in the Garden as a centrepiece. It was unveiled during the 11.00 a.m. Mass celebrated by Fr Caffrey with the choir singing Mozart's No. 2 Mass. Fr Lennon, the curate, preached on the Divinity of Christ and pointed out that the window showed three Catholic doctrines: commemorating dead relations, friends and benefactors, the propriety of honouring the saints, and the aim of the Catholic Church to gather everything beautiful in science and art round the altar. The press reported that the church was beautifully decorated for the Christmas solemnities with a banner bearing the words, *Gloria in Excelsis Deo* in an elevated position in the sanctuary, and across the choir balcony another proclaiming 'This day is born to you a Saviour'. (Luke 1:11)[8] During this period, as we shall see, the clergy took every opportunity in their sermons to propound Catholic doctrine, knowing that every word would be faithfully recorded by the press.

One most important part of St Mary's church that was still lacking, was the tower and spire that Pugin had included in his designs, and in 1888 Fr Caffrey set about rectifying this omission. In October the ceremony of laying the foundation stone took place – a stone with significance since it was obtained from the Abbey of St Mary of Furness (as was the first Catholic church in Ulverston), thereby provided the parishioners with a visible link connecting their church with its roots. The total height of the tower and spire was planned to be 150 feet when completed; it was also intended to house a peal of bells, though this was never achieved. Fr Caffrey himself laid the stone, but Fr Laverty, who had been instrumental in founding the infant Barrow mission was also in attendance. In his address, Fr Caffrey reminded the congregation of the progress of Barrow's Catholic population and its contribution to the town's religious and educational life; of the history of the mission and of the part Fr Laverty had played when he came each week from Ulverston, to celebrate Mass in 'the upper room'.[9] The work was completed in just under a year and the grand opening on 15 September 1889 was marked by a Solemn High Mass at which Bishop O'Reilly of Liverpool was the celebrant. The press, commenting on this occasion, remarked that the history of the Roman Catholic Church in

Barrow, and the vast strides it had made, resembled the history of Barrow itself. With the addition of the tower and the spire, the church now had three entrances, and over the doorway of the tower a statue of Our Lady.[10]

The last decade of the century saw a new sacristy built in 1894, the furniture being provided by Mr J. P. Smith, who also donated the Lady Altar in memory of his father.[11] (Mr Smith, an active parishioner, was to become mayor of Barrow in 1901 and again in 1911 and 1912.) The same year, 1894, Confessionals were added and an octagonal baptistry at the north-east corner; a single bell weighing 23cwt. was erected in the tower. After all these additions were complete the church was re-decorated and the re-opening celebrated in October with Solemn High Mass. In 1896 a new class-room and cloak-room were added to both the girls' and infants' schools, and Fr Caffrey, after many years' endeavour, succeeded in establishing a community of nuns in Barrow. In October 1897, six sisters of the Institute of the Sacred Heart of Mary arrived in Barrow and took up residence in a large building called Furness House in Nelson Street.[12] The sisters' work in Catholic education in Barrow is remembered to this day by the older members of the parish. Their work now is pastoral, catechetical and concerned with the hospital chaplaincy.

The century closed with the sudden death from pneumonia on 10 October 1899 of Fr Caffrey, at the early age of fifty-six.[13] His solemn funeral was conducted, with dirge chanted, the altar and sanctuary draped in black, his chalice, stole and biretta placed on his coffin and the requiem sung by the Bishop of Liverpool, accompanied by thirty-nine priests; anticipating the fuller development of ecumenical relations in the twentieth century, the service was attended by Anglican, Methodist and Presbyterian clergy, together with the mayor of Barrow and members of the Corporation – a fitting tribute to the respect both he and his community had won in the town at large during his ministry. This respect was shown by the number of people who, in spite of heavy rain, lined the entire route to the cemetery. Flags were flown at half-mast from the Town Hall and many other buildings; blinds were drawn in houses and buildings along the route, including St Matthew's vicarage. The hearse was followed by fifty-six coaches.[14]

The second half of the nineteenth century, during which Barrow became an incorporated borough in 1867, saw extraordinary strides made in its industrial and economic development and in the provision of public health, decent housing, education, and religious and cultural provisions. The social conditions in Barrow during this period were appalling; the lack of sewerage, with effluent from privies left to soak into the ground, was the cause of outbreaks of small-pox and cholera.[15] The Catholic population suffered its share of deaths, and, like the rest of the town, a high rate of infant mortality.[16] Barrow's education system, though, had a lot to thank St Mary's for. The opening of St Mary's school in August 1872, was anticipated with pleasure, in that it would fill, in some part, the pressing need of the town. The press deplored the fact that at that time hardly one third of the children of Barrow attended school, the result being idleness and misery. *The Barrow Herald* commented in its editorial: '"Beware of idleness," wrote St Benedict, "it is the greatest enemy of the soul."'[17] Indeed, St Mary's schools always received high praise from the school inspectors, even though in many cases the pupils' families were too poor to pay the small fee, and had to apply for assistance to the local Board of Guardians. Some of the parents of the girl pupils were unable to afford the material for sewing lessons, which had to be provided by the head-mistress.[18] The School Board set up under the Education Act of 1871, had the responsibility of providing schools, but were slow in providing sufficient schools promptly enough for the town's rising population so that hundreds of young people were continually hanging round the streets, annoying and insulting passers-by. Fr Caffrey had many battles with the School Board over finance in connection with St Mary's schools: denominational schools at that time received no financial help from the Board, but all rate-payers, including Catholics, had to pay the rate set for the Board schools. This general charge also applied to the Church of England schools.

While the town's Catholics were of necessity fully involved in these educational developments, their attention was also held by changes taking place in their Church, as its papal leadership lost its political and temporal power to what became during this period a united Italy. The problems of the pope and the Papal States were not at all 'remote' to our area's Catholics, for they were brought to the attention of St Mary's congregation by pastoral letters from Bishop Goss of Liverpool, in October 1866 and December 1867. On the purely religious front, as the Catholic Church underwent a powerful re-affirmation of the pope's spiritual authority at just the time when his secular power as an Italian ruler was being destroyed, Catholic Furnessians were made *au courant* with the work of the First Vatican Council in defining the Holy Father's infallibility: while the Council was in session, on 24 January 1869, Fr Bilsborrow gave a lecture entitled 'Supremacy of the Pope – Scriptural Proofs'.

While ecumenical developments lay largely in the future, the declaration of papal infallibility was undoubtedly a factor in distancing Catholics from Protestants in Victorian Britain. At the same time, the edge of controversy was whetted by the strong proselytising zeal of nineteenth-century British Catholics. The defence and promotion of the faith inspired in Furness a series of polemical and historical lectures/sermons delivered on Sunday evenings by Fr Bilsborrow in 1869 and 1870 on aspects of 'The Reformation'. Naturally, these declamations did not go unchallenged, and the Rev. W. Briscombe, a Methodist minister, started to give lectures countering Fr Bilsborrow. Not only were these polemical lectures reported in full, but correspondence columns of the papers were full of readers' comments, which at times became very heated. The battle came to an end in April 1870 by order of the editor of *The Barrow Herald*: religion clearly was very important to the inhabitants of Barrow in the nineteenth century, as it was to many, if not most, Victorian people. In spite of this fiery exchange of opinions in the press and the polemic lectures given, co-existent with them was a nascent ecumenism. In the early seventies Fr Bilsborrow was president of an adult-education centre with Sir. James Ramsden as chairman and at least one Church of England clergyman on the committee. When Fr

Bilsborrow's health failed in 1872, his resignation drew from Sir James an eloquent speech of regret and appreciation of the good work that he had done for the town.[19] This working partnership between the priests at St Mary's and the clergy of the other denominations continued and showed its full expression in their participation in Fr Caffrey's funeral.

At the same time the influence locally of the Anglo-Catholic Tractarian movement launched in the Church of England by John Keble (1792–1866), Edward Pusey (1800–1821) and John Henry Newman (1801–1890), though it aligned its proponents with the Catholic Church and its ritual, probably poisoned relations between Catholicism and the Protestant mainstream who faced the importations of 'popish' doctrines and practices into the Established Church. The Tractarians were to have a powerful effect on Barrow: the vicar of St George's, the Parish Church of Barrow, Rev. T. S. Barrett, was attracted to this movement and adjusted his services accordingly. This raised bitter correspondence in the local press, and in May 1867 objections by parishioners, countersigned by the Duke of Devonshire, Lord Frederick Cavendish, Mr H. Schneider, Mr James Ramsden and several others, all of whom had been, as we saw in Chapter 6, generous patrons of Catholic developments in the town, were made against the 'ritualistic' services and neo-Catholic doctrines held at St George's. Even the Cottage Hospital was involved, for Mr Barrett as hospital chaplain was responsible for a 'multiplicity of crosses' in the building, and 'lighted candles placed each side of a corpse and a cross at the head'.[20] These 'crosses' were most likely crucifixes.

The furore within Barrow Anglicanism was stepped up when a branch of the 'Confraternity of the Blessed Sacrament', formed within the Church of England by Anglo-Catholics to bring back Eucharistic devotion into their Church, was established in the town, with the vicar of St George's as a member. The editor of The Barrow Herald wondered what steps the bishop would take to deal with Mr Barrett, and in fact the Dean of Carlisle preached a sermon against ritualism and asked 'Do we want the Church to be Romish or Protestant?'[21] Things came to a head when a 'Memorial' was presented to the Bishop of Carlisle complaining about the performance of divine worship at St George's Church:[22] one comment was that this had become a 'Popish Masshouse', another, that worship at St George's was little different in form from that at St Mary's. On 8 October 1877 Mr Barrett, being ill, employed a locum to take the service; he was dressed in fact, as a Catholic priest, with 'biretta, amice, stole and chasuble', bowing to the altar, on which were lighted candles and crucifix. When the service began, the people's churchwarden, outraged, challenged the locum to produce a licence from the Bishop; none was forthcoming so the churchwarden shut the book in his face and called on the curate to take the service. Both clerics retired to the vestry, Mr Child, the curate donning the vestments discarded by Mr Ashworth; they both came out and concluded the service together, the congregation remaining quiet throughout. At last, the Bishop of Carlisle acted, sending Mr Barrett an injunction to refrain from using vestments. He complied, but when he was told to remove the crucifix from the altar he resigned, in December 1878, much missed by his like-minded congregation.[23] It would appear that Barrovians were quite tolerant of Catholicism, provided it remained safely within the walls of St Mary's church. What they objected to was any infiltration of 'Romish' ideas into the Established Church. Mr Barratt's resignation on the principle of the crucifix was very sad, since today St George's church has a resplendent life-size crucifix taking pride of place against the curtain, forming a reredos to the altar; such features reveal the extent to which Barratt's kind of Anglo-Catholicism is taken for granted in the modern Church of England.

The effect of the industrialisation centred on Barrow, especially that of ship-building in the latter part of the century, spilled over to increase the population of Ulverston. This heart-land of Furness Catholicism, whilst never matching the phenomenal expansion of Barrow, nevertheless saw a considerable increase in its population. When Fr Thomas Allan took charge of the Ulverston parish in 1877 he found the new school almost complete, but realised that the church in Fountain Street, built with the proceeds of the remaining Preston legacy, and having played such an important part in sustaining the link of Catholicism in Furness, had now become inadequate to accommodate the rising numbers of Catholics. Bishop O'Reilly's distress at the situation in Ulverston was made clear in his 1887 Advent Pastoral Letter:

> We have quite recently visited Ulverston and were struck by the miserable appearance of all the surroundings of the church in that town. It was a sad sight and a bitter reflection to think that the oldest mission in that large tract of country was in such a condition ... A new church is an imperative necessity ...[24]

Fr Allan rose to the occasion and in consequence a new church was planned, the foundation stone of which was laid on 15 August 1893, twenty-seven years after that of the daughter church in Barrow. The new church, in Victoria Road, adjacent to the new school, was opened in August 1895, also proudly bearing the dedication to St Mary of Furness.

Fr Allan became a well-known figure in the district, and was an extremely talented artist. He carved a new pulpit and painted a life-size copy of Leonardo's Last Supper. The Stations of the Cross and a very large paschal candlestick, carved in oak, were also his work, still to be seen in Ulverston St Mary's.[25] He, like Fr Bilsborrow, was also an adroit controversialist, entering into a series of exchanges with the Rev. Mr Bardsley, M.A., the vicar of Ulverston parish church. He did so with wit and mostly portraying himself as no more than a 'pastoral bucolic missioner in a laborious parish'.[26]

Ulverston, and the Manor Mission, which has played such a large part in our story of the Furness peninsula, must now of necessity, disappear from these pages. Although a prosperous market town, Ulverston, after its initial growth during the second half of the nineteenth century when an iron-works was built, never expanded in the same degree as Barrow, and its population remained fairly static until the second half of the twentieth century when the pharmaceutical giant, Glaxo, built its factory on the old iron-works site. In Chapter 6 we examined the expansion during the nineteenth century of the Catholic population in the whole area and hinterland of the Furness peninsula, which called for the building of churches at Coniston, Grange, Dalton, and in this chapter, the new and bigger church at Ulverston. The figures given for the Catholic population in these towns for the end of the nineteenth century and the beginning of the twentieth, show that the numbers remained virtually unchanged for 1899, 1900 and 1901, but by 1912 there was a marked decrease. In contrast, the Catholic population of Barrow over the same period increased.[27] It is possible that some of the Ulverston and Dalton Catholics gravitated to Barrow where there was easier access to work. As these figures show, the necessity to expand and build more churches in the rest of Furness did not arise, with one exception which will be dealt with later, whereas in Barrow, as we shall see, during the twentieth century there was a steady growth, and it is on that town and the growth of its Catholicism that we must now focus.

Notes

1. *Barrow Herald*, 13 May 1882.
2. Ibid., 30 Oct. 1883; 13 Nov. 1883.
3. Ibid, 24 May 1884.
4. *Catholic Family Annual* (1899).
5. St Begh was a seventh century legendary Irish nun who gave her name to St Bees (Cumbria). Because of her local associations she has been adopted as an English saint.
6. *Centenary Celebrations*.
7. Reuban O'Neill Pearson was one of a number of antiquarians who inquired into the origins of the Seven Sacrament window at St Anthony's chapel, Cartmel Fell mentioned in chapter 1, notes 20, 21.
8. *Barrow Herald*, 2 Jan. 1886.
9. Ibid., 20 Oct. 1888.
10. *Barrow News*, 21 Sept. 1889.
11. *Centenary Celebrations*.
12. Ibid.
13. *Barrow Herald*, 14 Oct. 1899.
14. Catholic Family Annual (1900).
15. *Barrow Herald*, 4 Nov. 1871; 10 Feb. 1872; 9 March 1872.
16. Ibid., 19 Oct. 1872; 6 Sept. 1873; 14 July 1877.
17. Ibid., 17 Aug. 1872.
18. Ibid., 6 Sept. 1873.
19. Ibid., 14 Sept. 1872.
20. Ibid., 13 June 1868.
21. Ibid., 31 May 1873; 14 June 1873.
22. Ibid., 7 Feb. 1877.
23. Ibid., 9 April 1881.
24. Ward and Warren, *The Manor Mission*, p. 44.
25. Ibid., p. 47.
26. 'Father Allan's First and Second Reply to Rev. Mr Bardsley' in *Historical Papers* (1903), privately bound collection of pamphlets in author's possession, to be deposited at the Talbot Library, Preston. (n.p.).
27. Figures calculated from statistics in *Catholic Family Annual* editions for 1899, 1900, 1901 and 1912.

CHAPTER EIGHT

The twentieth century – before Vatican II [1]

The twentieth century at large has seen the greatest changes in Catholic thought and practice since the sixteenth century; in this chapter we shall see this reflected, on our local level, as we continue to consider the history of St Mary's parish, Barrow, Furness's largest Catholic church, as typifying the history of Furness Catholics in an age of continuing industrial and demographic expansion both within the period of the world wars, and the aftermath. As far as Catholicism in Furness is concerned, this century naturally divides itself into two sections; the period prior to the Second Vatican Council (1962–5), and the decades since that important event in Church history. We shall also pay particular attention to the role of ecumenical understanding amongst Christians in Furness generally and Barrow in particular; and how the decrees of the Council affected this development.

As the history of the Barrow Catholic community in the nineteenth century closed with the death of Fr Caffrey, so the twentieth opened with Fr John Miller's coming from Douglas, Isle of Man, as parish priest of St Mary's. He found the parish in good heart, with a population of 5,255, catered for by the rich liturgical and para-liturgical programme typical of British Catholicism in that period of vibrant devotion: there were Masses on Sundays at 8.00, 9.30, and 11 am; Catechism and Instruction were provided at 2.30 p.m. and Rosary, Sermon and Benediction at 6.30pm. On Holy Days, Masses were at 5.00, 8.00 and 9.00 a.m.; with Rosary, Sermon and Benediction at 7.30pm. Weekday Masses were at 7.30 and 8 a.m.; with Rosary, Sermon and Benediction on Tuesdays and Thursdays at 7.30 p.m. Confessions were available every morning before Mass, after Thursday Benediction, and from 6 to 9.30 p.m. on Saturday evenings. There were Confraternities of the Children of Mary; a Young Men's Society; the 'Living Rosary'; and the Altar Society. It was indeed a spiritually thriving parish, typifying the rapid growth of Catholicism in the nineteenth century industrial town, which in turn encapsulated the new urban and industrial orientation of the Catholic Church in Victorian Britain.[2]

Fr Miller, following in the footsteps of his predecessors, made the extension of the mission in Barrow his priority. St Patrick's school-chapel had been built to minister to the Catholics on Barrow Island as a filiation of St Mary's, but in September 1900, on the Feast of the Nativity of the Blessed Virgin Mary, the Rev. John Barry came from St Joseph's, Peasley Green, St Helens and was installed as the parish priest of this new parish. This year saw further expansion in Barrow. It was felt that there were so many Catholics in the Marsh and Salthouse areas that another church would have to be built to serve them. To this end, a site was purchased on which to build a school-chapel, for the number of Catholic children attending non-Catholic schools was causing concern.[3] It was decided that this mission would be dedicated to the Sacred Heart and on 16 June 1901, Dr Whiteside, Bishop of Liverpool, laid the foundation stone amid a gathering of over 2,000 people. The building was completed and open for worship on 8 June 1902 and in August the first rector was appointed, Fr Laurence Kehoe, ordained only two years earlier – though the credit for getting the two missions firmly and autonomously established must go to Fr Miller.

This building meant more debt, which was shouldered by all the Catholics of Barrow, and was addressed by such events as a 'Grand Bazaar and Sale of Work' held in the Town Hall in September 1902, in aid of the Father Caffrey Memorial Schools, subsequently Sacred Heart school-chapel, in Lumley Street.

Fr Miller not only encouraged the spiritual devotions already existing in the parish, but also aimed to raise the standard of the liturgy, partly in line with the growing appreciation, as set out in Pius X's *Motu Proprio* (1903), of the older Gregorian plainsong music of the Church. On Good Friday 1900, Fr Miller sang the Passion, an innovation at St Mary's, where previously it had been said only. By the end of the nineteenth century St Mary's parish had grown to such an extent (Catholic population 5,255), that there were now two curates helping the parish priest: in 1901 they were Patrick Ryan and William Motherway. On Good Friday of that year the Passion was sung in parts by the three priests and on Holy Saturday Fr Motherway sang the *Exultet* and the Litanies with responses by the choir. On Easter Sunday, there was Solemn High Mass with Fr Miller as celebrant with the two curates as deacon and sub-deacon.[4] The revival of more ancient, less ornate and less concert-like forms of liturgical music also directly affected the choir of St Mary's and was instrumental in the teaching of simple plain chant in the schools; the *Missa de Angelis* became the chant most familiar to Catholics. Fr Miller enthusiastically implemented Pope Pius X's instruction and during this period of his pastoral ministry he made the liturgy his special interest.

As we have seen, the numerical expansion of Catholicism in nineteenth-century Furness was made possible only by large-scale Irish immigration. One unfortunate side-effect in Barrow was that Fr Miller's time at St Mary's was marred by Irish anti-English feeling among some of the parishioners who were members of a group called *The Hibernians*. Fr Miller was an Englishman and on St George's Day, 1908, he flew the flag of St George from the flagstaff. This so infuriated this strong Irish nationalist element in the parish that they boycotted the collection plate; some of the collectors even went on strike. It was a very divisive time for the parish, and sides were taken sharply. Fr Miller was a good and hardworking priest but there was apparently a clash of personalities as well as of nationalities at work in this collision. The upshot was that Bishop Whiteside threatened to place the parish under an interdict, involving locking the church and refusing the Sacraments to the parishioners. This was a very serious response, though arguably the dissident group were so intractable that this threatened suspension of religious provisions was the only weapon left in the bishop's armoury that would bring them to their senses. It did, but the unfortunate rift may have been one of the causes of Fr Miller's breakdown in health. He left St Mary's the same year on sick leave, and in 1909 went as rector to St Peter's at Ince near Wigan, where he stayed for three years, then to St Sylvester's, Liverpool, until 1913. He was again on sick leave until 1914 when he went as rector to St Peter's at Woolston until 1916. After that point Fr Miller does not appear in the Catholic Directory, having left the priesthood. His chalice bearing the inscription: 'Gift of the Manx Faithful 1899' remains at Woolston.[5] It is understood that he emigrated to Australia. However, although the bishop moved Fr Miller from St Mary's, he was not going to be blackmailed by the ultra-nationalist Irish element and his answer to them was to send as their next parish priest in 1908, not an Irish priest, as they would have wished, but the most English of English priests, Robert Dobson. Yet Fr Dobson was obviously more diplomatic than Fr Miller; he won over all hearts and became known affectionately by his parishioners as 'Dobby'.

Fr Dobson stayed as pastor at St Mary's, seeing the parish through the trauma of the Great War, until in 1922 he was raised to episcopal rank, consecrated bishop of Cynopolis (*in partibus infidelium*),[6] by Archbishop Keating of Liverpool on 30 November, and subsequently took up his appointment as auxiliary Bishop of Liverpool. Liverpool had been raised to the status of an archbishopric when Bishop Whiteside was appointed archbishop on 28 October 1911. During his period at St Mary's. Fr Dobson increased the number of sodalities by introducing the Holy Family Confraternity and the Guild of St Agnes. In 1904, Gerard Majella (1726–55), a Redemptorist lay brother, was canonised by Pius X and his cult quickly became popular. It was under Fr Dobson that a combined shrine to the honour of this saint and of Our Lady of Perpetual Succour was erected, containing a painting of the saint and a copy of the icon of Our Lady traditionally ascribed to St Luke. Placed, as it is, by the stairs to the organ loft, it still attracts much devotion. In 1910, on land owned by the church, a boys' club room was built and extensions in the church were made. Two flanking pedestals were added to the High Altar, with Gothic canopies in Caen stone to match the altar. The sanctuary was enlarged, and the pulpit brought within the sanctuary; the organ was reconstructed with pneumatic action and divided into two sections, so throwing open the view of the rose window which had previously been hidden. The whole church was painted and decorated by Messrs. Hardman and Company of Birmingham. The school also received attention, a new classroom being added to the boys' school.[7]

The continued demographic growth of the Catholic Church in industrial Furness induced the Archbishop of Liverpool, in 1915, to instruct Fr Dobson to establish a third parish in Barrow, looking to the catchment area roughly equivalent to the Anglican parishes of St Matthew's and St Paul's. Land was, clearly, at a premium in the Barrow of the First World War, one site, on the corner of Oxford Street and Clarence Road, being offered at £2,000. In the event the site was found unsuitable and the scheme for a third parish was still-born for the time being.[8]

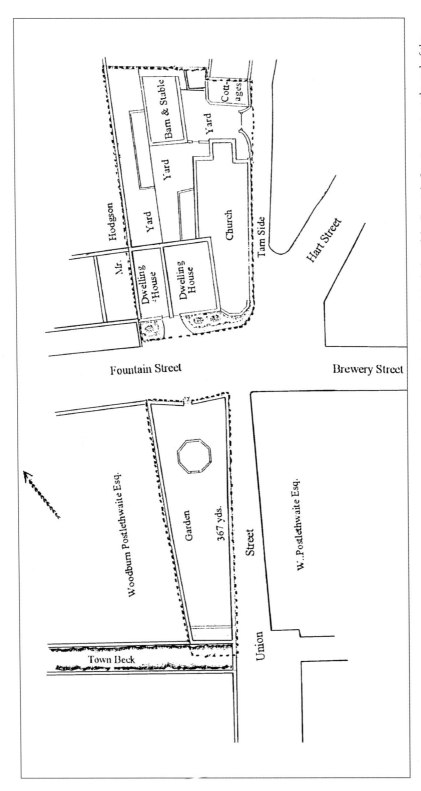

MAP 3. Plan of land acquired by Dr Everard and owned by the Catholic Church in Ulverston, showing the original plan of the Fountain Street property at the end of the eighteenth and the beginning of the nineteenth centuries. (*Reproduced by kind permission of the Archives of the Society of Jesus, Mount Street, London*)

In Ulverston, meanwhile, Fr Kehoe from the Sacred Heart parish, Barrow, followed Fr Allan who, it will be remembered from the previous chapter, made such a contribution to the Ulverston church, when he left the town in 1907. Fr Kehoe's main contribution to the Catholic community of Ulverston was to found, in 1913, the first 'conference' in the area of the charitable St Vincent de Paul Society. This lay society was instrumental in providing both Christmas breakfasts for the destitute children of the parish and going on to respond to the demands of the Great War by sending comforts for the soldiers serving abroad.[9] The number of Catholics in Ulverston was also increasing. Munitions work at Vickers in Barrow had attracted workers not only to Barrow but also to the whole of the surrounding Furness district. The community of nuns that Fr Caffrey had succeeded in bringing to Barrow proved of invaluable help in the education of the children of the town, both in the parish schools and in the private school held in their house in Nelson Street. Their teaching was so successful that Fr Kehoe, realising the need for a convent school in Ulverston, invited them to establish one in his parish. This opened its doors on 8 September 1913, in the face of still vigorous 'anti-popery' expressed by the rector of Ulverston, the Reverend J. H. Heywood. He issued 'a letter of warning to church and chapel parents', and although he acknowledged 'the outward charm, culture, quietness, and gentleness of these devout ladies', he was very uneasy at the idea of a Roman Catholic convent school in the town.[10] Fr Kehoe left Ulverston in 1915, to be followed by Fr Patrick Joseph Delaney.

When Fr Dobson, after his consecration as bishop in 1922, left St Mary's, he was followed by Fr Delaney, who like the first priest to serve St Mary's, came from Ulverston. Fr Delaney, later to become dean, was born in Kenmare, County Kerry, but had conducted his priestly studies at Ushaw College, and his first appointment was at St Peter's, Lancaster. While at Ulverston, he undertook to arrange the erection of the lychgate at the entrance to the church grounds, as a memorial to those men from the parish who had given their lives in the Great War. When he came to Barrow, one of his first priorities was to see that a memorial of some sort was built to honour the men from St Mary's who had fallen in the War. This took the form of a Memorial Club in Nelson Street. The schools now began to give concern; the buildings in which they were housed had been condemned by the Board of Education and they needed to be completely re-built. The cost for this major project was £10,000, and Fr Delaney carried the burden of this debt for the rest of his life.

After the Catholic Hierarchy was restored in 1850, Barrow was part of the diocese of Liverpool. By 1924 the population of the Catholic Church in the North of England had grown to such an extent that a new diocese of Lancaster was formed by taking part from Liverpool and part from Hexham and Newcastle and comprising the Hundreds of Amounderness and Lonsdale in Lancashire, and the counties of Cumberland and Westmorland. By the papal bull *Universalis Ecclesiae* of 22 November, 1924 the new diocese came into being. Thomas Wulstan Pearson, O.S.B., born in Preston in 1870, was appointed as first bishop on 18 December 1924 and consecrated by Archbishop Keating of Liverpool in St Peter's Church, Lancaster on Shrove

Tuesday, 24 February 1925. The Rt Rev. Joseph Butt, auxiliary to the Cardinal Archbishop of Westminster, the Rt Rev. Robert Dobson, auxiliary to the archbishop of Liverpool, Bishop Shine of Middlesborough, Bishop Cowgall of Leeds and Bishop Thorman of Hexham and Newcastle assisted.[11]

Furness Abbey celebrations

One of the most historic events that took place during Dean Delaney's period was the 800th anniversary of the founding of Furness Abbey in 1127. The whole of Furness took this event to their hearts. The Anglicans were rallied by the Bishop of Barrow, the Rt Rev. Herbert Sidney Pelham, who wrote, in a most ecumenical spirit to all his incumbents asking for help in the big effort to celebrate the founding of the Abbey. Bishop Pelham wrote:

> … We are proud of our great historic church; we thank God for the story of its ceaseless effort to promote the cause of Christ. The Cistercian monks, who built the Abbey in olden times, with their vows of chastity and poverty, rank high among our spiritual forefathers, and it is only right that we should look back with deep thankfulness for their true devotion.
>
> May, I therefore, ask all of you to keep Saturday, 16 July free from all engagements, personal and parochial … let us in Barrow and district show that we are truly thankful for the glories of the past as an inspiration to high endeavour in the future.[12]

The local press made much of this event and of the circumstances leading to the surrender of the Abbey. With regard to the propaganda put out by Henry VIII against the monks to excuse his actions, *The North Western Daily Mail* quoted Edmund Burke: 'An enemy is a bad witness, a robber is a worse.'[13]

On Saturday, 16 July, the Anglicans of the district celebrated the Abbey's history in grand style, although, unfortunately, because restoration work on the ruins was in progress, neither this nor the Catholic celebration could take place in the Abbey itself. Instead, it was held in the field adjacent, described as 'Abbey Park', now the 'Amphitheatre', where a service was conducted by the Bishop of Carlisle, the preacher being the bishop of Durham, Dr Hensley Hinson, a proponent of the continuity of the Anglican Church from pre-Reformation days. In fact it was the statement of these historical views, which, at a time when controversy, aroused by the Bull of Pope Leo XIII, *Apostolicae Curae* (1896)[14] over the validity of Anglican priestly orders which declared them to be 'completely null and void' (par. 36), and not in direct line from the medieval Church was still fresh, that upset the eirenic atmosphere so far prevailing: Hinson's sermon sparked a retort in the shape of a letter to the press from the Catholic parish priests of Barrow. This letter was also incorporated into the official pro-gramme for the Catholic celebration, it denied the continuity of the Anglican Church:

> … [discontinuity] is proved by their liturgy, the pivot of which, in

pre-Reformation times, was the Sacrifice of the Mass and the doctrine of transubstantiation. To claim continuity of faith and reject the Mass is a contradiction ... to defend this dogma we Catholics have endured heavy penalties, cruel persecution, social ostracism, political disability – this is the price our forefathers paid for their loyalty to the Old Faith and the Mass.

The Barrow priests went on to refer to a remark culled from the *Church Times* with which they fully agreed: 'Anglicans have a legal and constitutional continuity; Romans a continuity of doctrine, worship and discipline.' The spirit of controversy now aroused was deplored, but nevertheless continued, by the Bishop of Barrow. In contrast, a wise statement put out by Archbishop Cosmo Gordon Lang of York, echoed the ecumenical mood set by the Bishop of Barrow himself in his initial call for a positive Anglican response to the centenary celebrations. Archbishop Lang's words can, indeed, be read as pointing forward to the later realisation of ecumenical goals in Furness with the setting up in Barrow of a *Council of Churches*, now *The Churches Together in Barrow*:

> ... There is something very wearing in the procession of mere assertion and counter-assertion. It is not in this way that truth is reached. There is need rather of patient and fair-minded study, of thinking freely and without prejudice; above all, of taking pains to understand each other. Mutual understanding is the first step in that cause of the unity of all Christian people to which everyone who understands Christ's will and his purpose for his Church is bound to be loyal. And if as it often seems, some differences remain, deep and irreconcilable, there also remains the call of Christian charity.[15]

The Catholic celebration took place on Thursday, 21 July 1927. More than 10,000 people attended; two special trains came from Whitehaven and Millom and joined with others coming from Preston and Manchester. Without question, it was the largest and most spectacular demonstration of its kind ever witnessed in Furness and even merited inclusion in 'Movietone News'. Cardinal Bourne, Archbishop of Westminster, came on the Wednesday and for that purpose an oriel window was installed at St Mary's presbytery to enable him to address the crowds from his bedroom window and give his blessing. On the Thursday morning the procession began from Ramsden Square, consisting of forty individual items, including many tableaux. In five carriages rode the cardinal, four bishops (including Bishop Dobson), the Benedictine abbots of York and Ampleforth, senior clergy of the diocese, the mayor, Alderman Ellison, the High Sheriff, Colonel Sir J. P. Reynolds, and Commander Charles Craven (retired R.N. and Managing Director of Vickers Armstrongs Limited). The clergy of the diocese, Benedictine monks and Catholic men of the town and diocese followed on foot. Ceremonies began at 11.00 a.m. with the Bishop of Lancaster, the Rt Rev. Mgr Pearson, O.S.B., as celebrant. The bishop began by intoning the opening versicle from the Office of Terce, then proceeded to vest while the Office was continued according to the monastic breviary by the choir of

Benedictine monks from Ampleforth. The Mass was that of the Holy Ghost. The Cardinal preached to the effect:

> ... that the purpose of the celebration was to offer once again the Sacrifice of the Mass in thanksgiving to God for 400 years of incessant prayers that went up from that spot; in reparation for the outrage committed 400 years ago and to draw from the celebrations courage and inspirations for the future. Old lies that used to be taught in all our schools to justify the dissolution of the monastery were recognised as lies today and the most that any man could say was that these monks had outlived their usefulness.

The Cardinal's standpoint was rather less defensive *vis-à-vis* the monks than the comments made by Dr Goss, Bishop of Liverpool, when preaching at the opening of St Mary's church in 1867. Unfortunately, the weather was not kind to those in attendance: the heavens opened and Benediction of the Blessed Sacrament, which it was intended should follow Mass, had to be cancelled.

At a civic reception at the Town Hall given by the mayor for Cardinal Bourne, ecumenical aims were once again to the fore. The mayor, after welcoming the Cardinal, and commenting that this was the first time a Cardinal had visited Barrow, informed him that there were representatives of every Christian Church in Barrow present at this occasion. Alderman Ellison, speaking of the Barrow Catholics as citizens, 'wished to say that the happiest relationship existed between them and the rest of the community, and that they were particularly proud in Barrow of the fact that there was no religious bigotry or intolerance in the town, and difference

FIGURE 16. Cardinal Bourne at the front door of St Mary's Presbytery on the occasion of Furness Abbey's 800th anniversary celebrations. (*By kind permission of Sankeys*)

FIGURE 17.
Furness Abbey 800th anniversary celebrations. (*By kind permission of Sankeys*)

of belief did not in any way interfere with their provision of social services'. The cardinal replied, congratulating the mayor on the municipal life of the town and remarked that 'what they had witnessed that day made them realise that, whatever the differences there were of old, the breaches in the churches was not regarded as something dividing the history of the country into two separate parts'. He thought that when the next centenary came they would be united in more things than they were at the time of speaking. This was greeted by applause.[16] Thus, happily, the outcome of the Furness Abbey commemoration, an occasion with a strong potential to divide, was in the event unitive and pointed towards the great gains made towards church unity in the region as the twentieth century proceeded.

Catholic education expands

The Institute of the Sisters of the Sacred Heart of Mary had served both the parish and the town since they came in Fr Caffrey's time. Since then they had expanded their private convent school from their house in Nelson Street to premises in Holker Street, now occupied by the *British Legion*. In 1923–24 the Sisters bought Crosslands House on the outskirts of the town and moved to this mansion with extensive grounds, sufficient land, in fact, to build a new convent secondary school. Unfortunately, things did not go as planned; for as the Superior, Sr. Mary Nativity reported to the bishop in December 1927, the Barrow Education Committee had decided 'that there is adequate accommodation for Secondary Education in the town already', and had therefore 'put a stop to our proposed new Secondary School'.[17] The objection was finally overcome and the building went ahead in 1928; the new Secondary School, named 'Our Lady's' which served the whole of Furness as far as Coniston, opened in September 1929. The Sisters then closed the small establishment they had continued to run in Ulverston. In Barrow they continued to serve the cause of Catholic education in the elementary schools of St Mary's, St Patrick's, Sacred Heart, and subsequently, the still to be built schools of the Holy Family and St Columba's parishes. By the 1950s, the need for a Catholic comprehensive school became apparent, and a large site was acquired in close proximity to the ruins of Furness Abbey. This school, dedicated to St Aloysius, the patron saint of youth, was built to cater for Catholic youth of both sexes, opening September 1954.

The consecration of the church

Although Dean Delaney had been struggling with the debt outstanding on the church and also with the heavy burden of having to re-build the schools, he managed to free the church from debt by 1931 and was therefore in a position to approach the bishop and arrange for St Mary's to be consecrated. This took place on Thursday, 28 May 1931, when Bishop Pearson came to conduct the ceremonies. It was a long morning, for the ceremonies began at 9am. and continued until well past 1pm, in a long and involved rite including the solemn procession of the relics of SS. Illuminatus and Leatantia (two of the early Christian martyrs) which were eventually placed in the sepulchre of the altar.[18] To mark the occasion, a very fine banner was commissioned, the design based on the seal of Furness Abbey. On the back of the banner a text most applicable to the occasion was inscribed, taken from the Coucher Book of the abbey:

> 'Mater Virgo pia, titulo, Domus ista Maria,
> Est tua dos propria, sua sis rectrix ope dia'

which may be translated 'O gentle Mother, Virgin Mary, this house, by dedication, is thine own dowry; may'st thou by divine aid be its benefactress.' (Translation by Paul V. Kelly.)[19] The banner now rests against the north wall of the St Patrick's shrine, adding to the embellishment of the church and giving witness to our succession from the Abbey Church of St Mary of Furness.

The consecration of the church was the last contribution that Dean Delaney made to the parish, for on Friday, 8 January 1932 the parish was saddened to learn of his untimely death under surgery. Among the many tributes to the dean a letter from the vicar of St James, and Joint Secretary of the Council of Churches, the Rev. R. William Stannard, to the editor *of The North-West Evening Mail*, fittingly singled out Fr Delaney's contribution to the ongoing development of the ecumenical cause in Barrow. He wrote

> I should like to place on record ... Dean Delany's [sic] generosity of outlook; he gladly accepted the position of vice-president of the Barrow Council of Churches from its inception, and was an active chairman of one of its groups.[20]

The attendance at Fr Delaney's requiem by the rural dean and vicar of St George's, the vicar of St James, as well as by a minister representing local Nonconformity, provided further testimony to his work in inter-church relations.[21]

Dean Delaney's successor was Canon Edward Tuohey, a learned priest whose investigations showed that although the original title of the church

FIGURE 18.
Laying the found-
ation stone of Scared
Heart new church,
Barrow. The old
school chapel seen in
the background was
replaced in 1929.
(*By kind permission
of Sankeys*)

and parish was simply 'St Mary's', over the course of time the honorific appellation 'of Furness' had become generally accepted.[22] The unofficial adoption by the Catholic churches both in Barrow and Ulverston of the appellation 'St Mary of Furness' reveals the strength of the hold that the medieval abbey continued to exercise over Catholic imaginations in Furness down to the present day.

Owing to ill, health Canon Tuohey was moved to the small pilgrimage parish of Fernyhalgh, near Preston in 1937; his replacement was Fr Joseph McKenna, M.B.E. who was, on his appointment, made dean of the Furness district. Joseph McKenna had been ordained in 1915 and had spent the rest of the war as an army chaplain, including service in Salonika. After hostilities ceased, he went to Fleetwood and whilst there, in 1927, in recognition of his unremitting rescue work during the great gale and flood that hit the town in that year, he was awarded the M.B.E. Dean McKenna was an expert on the history of Catholic education and served for twenty years as chief inspector of religious education in the diocese.[23]

When Joseph McKenna came to Barrow the storm clouds of war were once more beginning to gather, and he led the parish in intensive prayer that war would be averted: the first effects of the war were felt in Furness with the bombing of Barrow, first in April 1941 and then with a heavy blitz in May. In the May bombardment the Baptist church in Abbey Road was destroyed and several of the other Barrow churches suffered damage. On the weekend of the 3–4 May most of the damage was done; worshippers going to the first Mass on Sunday found St Mary's church ankle deep in rubble and debris, the pews thick with dust, though still standing and apparently untouched: in fact, unknown at the time, the whole of the roof had been lifted and then replaced by the blast of the bombs.

Church building in Barrow

Although the war meant that many Barrovians were called up into the armed services, and the death toll from the blitz was not inconsiderable, the town experienced economic prosperity and a demographic expansion through the increased work-force needed for the arms trade. Destroyers, aircraft-carriers, submarines and armaments were being produced as Barrow's war effort. In the post-war economic recovery Vickers' order books remained full: the growing demand for surface vessels, especially oil-tankers, and the need to replace shipping lost in the war, brought prosperity to the town. The consequent increase in population sustained during the war and post-war period, and the need to make good the freeze on house-building during wartime created a boom in house building in the private sector, but also a vast programme of council house building was undertaken which occasioned a shift in the location of population. There was a tendency towards an evacuation from the town centre towards the outskirts.

The Church authorities addressed this situation first on Walney Island, where, since 1916 the Catholics had been served by a small wooden building which acted as school during the week and a chapel on Sundays. This was a succursal chapel of St Patrick's church, but in 1949 it became a parish in its own right, the first parish priest being Fr W. Lennon, Ph.D. In 1957 and again in 1962 the school was extended to accommodate not only the children of Walney but also those from Barrow Island, St Patrick's schools having closed. A new church worthy of the parish was built in 1958 dedicated to St Columba.

By 1950 both private and council sector housing in the South Newbarns area had grown owing to the increased affluence and population growth of the town, and also by the building of a large council housing estate. The

FIGURE 19.
High altar, St Mary of Furness, Barrow, before re-ordering.

FIGURE 20.
High altar, St Mary of
Furness, Barrow, as
re-ordered after
Vatican II. (*By
courtesy of the* North
West Evening Mail)

provision of both church and school was needed and this was catered for
in 1951 by the building of a church dedicated to The Holy Family, to be
closely followed by the provision of a school.

The area of North Newbarns, that had given the Archbishop of Liverpool
such concern in 1915, when he had enquired into the possibility of purchasing land in Oxford Street, and which now extended to include the residential
districts of Hawcoat and Ormsgill, had been served, during the war years,
by the provision of Sunday Mass in the Catholic chapel in the cemetery
from 1941, and later in Romney Hall (George Romney's early home), Quarry
Brow, Hawcoat. By December 1948, Dean McKenna (by now Canon

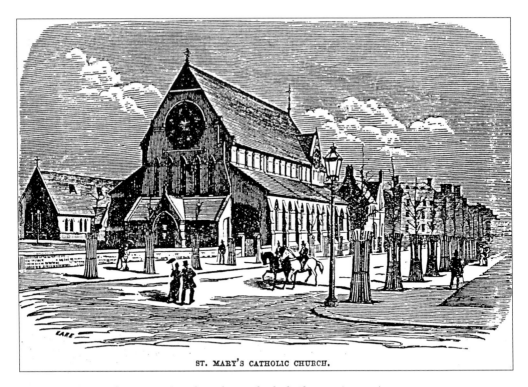

ST. MARY'S CATHOLIC CHURCH.

McKenna, having been appointed to the Cathedral Chapter in 1942), was beginning a long battle to acquire land for a church at Ormsgill: in 1952 he sent a memorandum to the bishop to the effect that land he had in mind at Ormsgill was subject to a public enquiry because of 'objections by the Furness Brick and Tile Company who require the land for minerals'.[24] [This was boulder clay]. Finally, in 1957 a plot at Ormsgill was bought and a church, dedicated to the newly canonised St Pius X, was opened. The need was desperate, for a council housing estate had been built at Ormsgill to cater, to a large extent, for the slum clearance and the re-housing needed as a result of the bombing in the Hindpool area which had housed many of St Mary's parishioners. This estate acquired the soubriquet 'Vatican City' owing to the high proportion of Catholics living there. At first the new church had to be served from St Mary's until, in 1958 the first priest, Fr Leo Cafferty took up residence. Eventually a school was built to accommodate the large number of Catholic children on the estate, and also for those from Hindpool, St Mary's schools having by now closed. Mass ceased to be celebrated at Romney Hall and St Pius X's church catered for both the Ormsgill estate and the private sector housing in North Newbarns and Hawcoat.

Canon McKenna contributed to adult education by holding meetings for the men of the area to study the Church's social teachings, as expressed in the second papal social encyclical *Quadragesimo Anno* published by Pope Pius XI in 1931, forty years after Leo XIII's *Rerum Novarum*. Canon McKenna had strong feelings on communism, contraception, and divorce which he looked on as the chief evils of the time. In fact, he had the amazing

FIGURE 21.
Exterior of St Mary of Furness, Barrow, prior to the addition of the tower and spire.

ability, no matter what the text of his sermon, to be able to bring all three into his exhortation. One member of his congregation called them 'the three Cs' – communism, contraception and connubial infelicity – and would mentally tick them off as each in turn was mentioned. He always scored full points! At the end of Canon McKenna's life, when this same parishioner was visiting him at Boarbank Nursing Home, he plucked up courage and told him about 'the three Cs'. Canon McKenna, who had mellowed by then, saw the joke, laughed, and said that if he had still been in a position to preach, instead of being retired, he would have added another 'C' now, this time a positive one – co-operation.

The sign of things to come

The Second World War saw a marked acceleration of the Catholic Church's adaptation to the relentless demands of an industrial economy, not least one involved in total war, in a munitions town such as Barrow. In May 1945 *The North-West Evening Mail* reported an unusual occurrence in St Mary's church when at 5.35 p.m. on the evening of 2 May:

> Men wearing hobnailed boots and stained with the dust of the day's toil entered. For centuries the rule had been that Mass be said no later than one hour after noon. And yet, a Mass was being celebrated in the evening, the Feast of the Ascension – a Holy Day of Obligation. Pope Pius XII, acting on the Catholic principle that 'It is the Mass that matters', and recognising that for many, morning Mass was impossible or difficult, relaxed the rule. More than 400 people attended last night's first evening Mass in a Barrow Catholic church.[25]

This dispensation applied only to Masses on Holy Days, and Catholics had to wait until 1956 for a Sunday evening Mass; but there were even greater surprises in store, it was prophetic in foreshadowing the changes in Vatican II.

The centenary of St Mary of Furness

The year 1965 was a very important one for Canon McKenna, named a Domestic Prelate by Pope Paul VI at the instance of Bishop Foley in recognition of his services to the diocese, and thus acquiring the title of *monsignore*: but he also had the honour of being the parish priest while St Mary's celebrated its centenary. It was a hundred years since the parish had been officially established, in a paint shop. Now it was fitting that parishioners should celebrate and give thanks for the efforts of their parents, grand-parents and great-grandparents in achieving the daunting task of raising the money to build their fine church.

The celebrations began on Sunday, 27 June with a children's Mass in church, followed at 4.00 p.m. by High Mass at Craven Park Rugby League ground in the presence of the Rt Rev. Thomas B. Pearson, titular bishop of Sinda, and auxiliary bishop of Lancaster, with Mgr Canon McKenna as celebrant, Canon Henry Tootell of Cockermouth (a previous curate at St

Mary's) as deacon, and Fr G. Bilsborrow from The Holy Family church as sub-deacon. Among the congregation of over 3,000 were former curates of St Mary's, priests of the deanery; members of St Mary's Scout Troop, St Mary's Club and the Knights of St Columba. The choir was formed by students from St Mary's school, Our Lady's convent school and St Aloysius' school. The final blessing was given by Bishop Pearson.

Following the Mass there was a reception for the Bishop, in the Banqueting Hall, Barrow Town Hall, at which 280 parishioners and guests sat down to a reception tea, the mayor, Alderman Tyson, paying tribute to the respect in which the Catholic community was held, and to the part played by the Catholic councillors who had put Catholic teaching into practice when serving the community. Bishop Pearson then congratulated St Mary's on reaching its century and told the parishioners that there was a noble breed among the Catholics of Barrow, and although fewer in number than those of Preston, they ranked equally with them in their strength of Catholicism. He commented that a hundred years before, the total number of parishioners was only 275 and he was sure that they would have been surprised at the numbers attending the Centenary Mass.[26]

The celebrations continued for a week. On Tuesday, 29 June there was a social evening, tea and concert for the senior citizens of the parish in the school hall. On Thursday, 1 July a parish dinner was held in the public hall and on Saturday, 3 July a requiem Mass for the deceased priests and members of the parish of St Mary of Furness was celebrated at 11am. The week's celebrations came to a grand conclusion with a High Mass of thanksgiving on Sunday, 4th July at 11am, followed by a 'beat night' for the teenagers from 7.30 p.m. until 10.30 p.m.

It was well that Canon McKenna enjoyed these celebrations and received the honour of becoming a *monsignore* when he did, for his health began to fail and in 1966 he entered Boarbank Nursing Home, resigned his parish in 1967, and after a long illness died at Boarbank Hall, in the care of the Augustinian Nursing Sisters, on January 16th, 1969. Apart from the overt good works, few realised how much covert charitable work he did, especially with unmarried mothers. This he kept secret, owing to the confidentiality of the cases.[27] Perhaps the most poignant proof of his typically unpublished generosity came when he died: it was found that the plot of land that he had purchased for his grave ten years previously was already occupied; he had given it to two poor parishioners unable to buy a grave. He was buried in the grave already occupied by another Barrow priest.[28] Canon McKenna came back home to St Mary's, as was only right, for his requiem. The Mass was concelebrated by the Rt Rev. Brian Foley, Bishop of Lancaster, Fr Joseph McKenna, a nephew, and five priests associated with St Mary's. Evidence of the esteem in which Canon McKenna was held by his brother priests was shown by the number who struggled through the fog that enveloped that part of the diocese south of Shap, and also the number of civic representatives who attended, including the mayor.

Looking back over the hundred years since the foundation of the Catholic mission in Barrow, one can see a development in microcosm of the nineteenth century Catholic renewal in England – called by Newman 'The

FIGURE 22.
Exterior of St Mary of
Furness, Barrow,
1997.(*By courtesy of
the* North West
Evening Mail)

Second Spring'. More particularly, the history of Catholicism in Barrow
during this period is a vignette of similar developments in industrial towns
throughout England. The advances in science and industry vivified the
economy of the country in general, with consequences fully evident in
Barrow, a town which owed its existence to the Industrial Revolution.
Barrow's famous 'mushroom' development brought about such an increase
in population that inevitably swelled the local Catholic community; but
this was a Catholicism highly coloured by the Irish immigrants. The registers
of births and deaths in particular show, by their names, very few indigenous
Catholics. There were a few certainly, but these were mostly from the
hinterland of Furness where, almost unbelievably, some of the country

people had kept the Old Faith alive. Among the many English names
included in the Ulverston Baptismal registers for the early part of the
nineteenth century is to be found: Winstanley and Mercer. In 1812, Ann
and Walter Rosser, had a daughter baptised with Edward Mostyn Esq. and
Lady Mostyn as sponsors. The Knipe family, descendants of the old recusants and royalists of Rampside, by this time living on the east shore of
Lake Windermere at Low Wood, had two sons baptised at Ulverston, one
in 1835 and the other in 1838.[29]

FIGURE 23.
Centenary
celebrations of St
Mary of Furness,
Barrow. Mass
celebrated on Craven
Park rugby ground
with Bishop Flynn
preaching, Sunday 27
June 1965. (*By
courtesy of the* North
West Evening Mail)

In the aftermath of Catholic Emancipation in 1829, as has been shown
in chapter five, a certain feeling of inter-Christian embattlement existed
and continued in Furness during the decades of the nineteenth century.
Lines were drawn, doctrinal differences emphasised and history never
forgotten, as shown in the reaction of the rector of Aldingham to this piece
of legislation as related in Chapter 5. As also evident in the controversies
aired in public lectures and in the correspondence columns of the local
press. The faith of the Catholic community was extremely strong. However,
in spite of this, it is interesting to note that the relations between the parish
priests of St Mary's and both the civic personalities and the pastors of other
denominations were generally cordial. Fr Bilsborrow, the first parish priest
of St Mary's, Barrow, had been chairman of an ecumenical group formed
to encourage further education, and when he had to leave Barrow on health
grounds, the committee expressed deep sorrow on losing him. An ecumenical spirit was always present: a Catholic priest was always a member,
first, of the Board of Education, and then of the Borough Council's

Education Committee (until Barrow ceased to be a county borough, in 1974). The outstanding response and sympathy of all the town at Fr Caffrey's funeral and again when Fr Delaney died, showed a remarkable example of a town that showed little bigotry. In Barrow, formal ecumenism had begun as early as the 1920s, for we have the evidence of Fr Delaney's being vice-president of the *Barrow Council of Churches* from its inception. Unfortunately that date is not available. The letter from the Rev. R. William Stannard giving this evidence is a precious document; the fact that the *Council of Churches* existed in Barrow so long ago needs to be restored to the memories of the present members of that body. Ecumenism in Furness still had a long way to go, but its growth between 1865 and 1965 was remarkable.

Notes

1. Michael Walsh, *An Illustrated History of The Popes Saint Peter to John Paul II* (London: Marshall Cavendish Editions, 1980), pp. 206–11.
2. Sheridan Gilley, 'The Roman Catholic Church in England 1780–1940', in Sheridan Gilley and W. J. Sheils (eds), *A History of Religion in Britain. Practice and Belief from Pre-Roman Times to the Present* (Oxford and Cambridge Mass.: Blackwell, 1994), ch. 18.
3. *Catholic Family Annual*, 1901, p. 52.
4. Spiritual Diary kept in *Catholic Family Annual* for 1899, 1900 and 1901 by author's father.
5. B. Plumb, *Found Worthy* (Warrington: B. Plumb, 1986), p. 170.
6. (In the lands of the unbelievers). Those bishops whose relationship to their see must be titular, such as auxiliaries, are assigned a former residential see which has fallen into disuse. This designation was abolished by Pope Leo XIII, in 1882, and they are now known as 'titular'.
7. *Catholic Family Annual*, 1912, p. 57.
8. Letter from Fr R. Dobson to Archbishop of Liverpool, 11 May 1915, *Lancaster Diocesan Archives*, File: 'St Mary's, Barrow'.
9. Ward and Warren, *The Manor Mission*, p. 49.
10. Ibid., p. 50.
11. *North Western Daily Mail*, 24 Feb. 1925.
12. *Barrow Guardian*, 4 June 1927.
13. *North Western Daily Mail*, 9 July 1927.
14. Stephen G. Pearson, *Apostolicae Curae (1896): Its reception in Britain (1896–1897), and the theological issues arising from it.* A Paper presented in Partial fulfilment of the requirements for the S.T.B. (Unpublished thesis, Katholieke Universiteit, Leuven, 1989) In this paper the hopes for unity between the Roman Catholic and the Anglican Churches striven for by Viscount Halifax and a French priest, Fernand Portal, are discussed. Their hopes were dashed by the publication of this papal bull. Its reception in England by both Churches is well documented.
15. *North Western Daily Mail*, 16 July 1927.
16. *Barrow Guardian*, 23 July 1927.
17. Letter from Sr. M. Nativity to Bishop of Lancaster, 5 December 1927, in *Lancaster Diocesan Archives*, File: 'St Mary's, Barrow'.
18. *North Western Daily Mail*, 28 May 1931.
19. Paul V. Kelly, *St Mary's Banner*, Leaflet in B.R.L. (Lc200FC/Ban, Mary).

20. *North Western Daily Mail,* 11 Jan. 1932.

21. Ibid., 13 Jan. 1932.

22. Letters from Canon Tuohey to Bishop of Lancaster and reply, 22 March 1933, 23 March 1933, in *Lancaster Diocesan Archives,* File: 'St Mary's, Barrow'.

23. *Lancaster Diocesan Directory,* 1970, obituary, pp. 125–7.

24. Memorandum from Canon McKenna to Bishop of Lancaster, 24 March 1952, in *Lancaster Diocesan Archives,* File: 'St Mary's, Barrow'.

25. *North Western Evening Mail,* 3 May 1945. For further references to liturgical changes see Walsh, *The Popes,* p. 215.

26. *North Western Evening Mail,* 28 June 1965.

27. Known to the author through personal field-work with the Catholic Protection and Rescue Society, now Catholic Social Services.

28. *Lancaster Diocesan Directory,* 1970, obituary. pp. 125–27.

29. CRS, *Ulverston Registers,* p. 14.

CHAPTER NINE

The twentieth century – Vatican II onwards [1]

The impact of the vast transformations in government, liturgy and socio-political involvement of the Catholic Church set in motion by the Second Vatican Council (1962–5) was felt most immediately throughout the Church's countless parishes in the domain of congregational worship, where change included the introduction of 'bidding prayers' and the sign of peace, the considerable expansion of Scripture readings (to be delivered by lay people), the celebration of Mass with the priest facing the congregation, and perhaps most striking, the use of the vernacular throughout the Mass. (Sacrosanctum concilium, December 1963).[2] In Barrow, and following the departure of Canon McKenna in 1967, the main task of implementing the Council's decrees fell on the shoulders of Fr Robert Bickerstaffe, who strongly encouraged, for example, the role of lay, including women, readers of the Scripture passages in the 'The Liturgy of the Word'.

Catholic involvement in Ecumenism in Furness

Included in the Vatican Council's agenda of what its creator, Pope John XXIII called *aggiornamento* – bringing the Church up to date – was a serious commitment to ecumenism, as set out in the Council's decree *Unitatis redintegratio* of November 1964.[3] As far as Barrow was concerned, there was, as we have seen, a tradition of ecumenism going back to Dean Delaney in the 1920s, a tradition which continued in an unstructured form into the '40s when the various Churches in the town formed a Christian Action Group of which Chad Varah, the founder of the *Samaritans*, at that time curate at St John's church, Barrow Island, was one of the founders. Canon McKenna became associated with it and at first the group prayed together in silence. Later a meeting was held in 1939, at the King's Hall, Barrow, under the auspices of an ecumenical movement *The Sword of the Spirit*, and Canon McKenna received permission from the bishop for the Catholics to join with the rest present at the meeting, in prayer. However, a ban imposed in 1940 by the hierarchy of England and Wales on prayer with Protestants obviously formed a serious stumbling block to ecumenical endeavours. This had been imposed in response to a spontateous reciting of the Lord's Prayer at a meeting of *The Sword of the Spirit* (subsequently the *Catholic Institute for International Relations*) held at the Stoll Theatre, London, in 1940.[4] A further example of the suspicious nature of official Catholic attitudes to inter-church relations at that time comes in the circumstances of the early 1940s, when Mgr McKenna was invited as a speaker at one of the weekly Men's Fellowship meetings at Abbey Methodist Church, whereupon great care had been taken to choose 'Praise to the Holiest in the Height' as the hymn which would preceed the meeting. Surely, it was thought, one of Cardinal Newman's hymns would be acceptable, but Canon McKenna was bound by discipline not to enter the room until the hymn and prayers were over.[5]

Vatican II changed all that and a new freedom emerged, though alterations came about gradually, rather than rapidly. In 1963, the various denominations in Barrow, though with the exception of the Catholics, decided that they wished to form a *Council of Churches* (the previous one evidently having become defunct) and on December 6th 1963, they held their inaugural meeting at St Paul's School. At the first Annual General Meeting on 13 March 1964, eight months before the opening of Session 5 of the Vatican II Council which produced the Conciliar Decree on Ecumenism, Canon McKenna was present and expressed the goodwill of the Roman Catholic community and its desire to participate in as much of the work of the *Council of Churches* as possible.[6] At an executive meeting a month later, it was decided that Roman Catholic representatives should be invited to participate in activities of the *Council*. By early 1967, the Catholics must have still been dragging their heels, since no representative had come forward. However, by December 1967 arrangements were being made for the Week of Prayer for Christian Unity (which closes on the feast of the Conversion of St Paul, 25 January); this was an inter-church observance introduced originally in France in 1935, and Fr McGough, of the Sacred Heart parish agreed to conduct the main service of the week, while Fr Whelan, of St Patrick's accepted the invitation to become a representative on the *Barrow and District Council of Churches*, and was immediately voted on to the committee of the World Human Rights Year (1968).[7] At a *Council* meeting in February 1968 a welcome was given to three Roman Catholic representatives; no official response having come from the hierarchy, these representatives of the Catholic community could act only as official observers rather than as full participants at this and subsequent meetings. However, at the September meeting of the *Council*, in 1968, a statement was read from the Roman Catholic Ecumenical Commission of England and Wales concerning the ways in which Catholic members of local councils could participate in activities of councils of churches. Meanwhile, during the Weeks of Christian Unity, one of the three services was regularly held in one of the town's Catholic churches. Then, in 1970, at the Annual General Meeting of the town's *Council of Churches*, Frs. Bickerstaffe and Ainsworth were welcomed as full members of the *Council*. Ever since then, the Catholics have played their full part in co-operating with all the other Churches in the town, Fr Bickerstaffe being elected chairman in 1975.[8] Since 1970 there have been five Catholic chairmen of the local *Council of Churches*.

It was not only Barrow that showed an interest in the ecumenical movement in Furness. Ulverston and District had also formed their own *Council of Churches* and Fr Moxham was welcomed as a member representing the Catholics of Ulverston on 7 May 1969. Originally this group covered a large area of the countryside surrounding Ulverston, from

Urswick to Kirkby, also providing a Christian social focus in Ulverston with a coffee shop, the Catholics being active workers in this project. In 1990, it was decided that the area covered was too unwieldy and that the newly named *Ulverston Churches Together* should concentrate solely on Ulverston. Dalton had originally been part of the *Barrow and District Council of Churches*, but in September 1968 they became autonomous. Dalton, a smaller and more compact community, found it easier to take the further step in inter-church relations; becoming, on 30 November 1987, a formal *Local Ecumenical Partnership* bringing Anglicans, Catholics, and Free Churches into a covenanted partnership.[9] In Barrow also, there was the same further step towards greater unity, and in 1997, the churches on the Island of Walney also formed a *Local Ecumenical Partnership* in which Anglicans, Catholics, Methodists and Baptists are partners. In 1990, when the national body, *The British Council of Churches* became *The Churches Together in England and Wales*, with the Catholic Church in England taking a more active role, the opportunity was taken to change the local name from *The Barrow Council of Churches* to *The Churches Together in Barrow*.

It was Fr Bickerstaffe who began the tradition of holding the ecumenical Pentecost service at Furness Abbey, and Whit Sunday 1976 saw all the Churches, of Barrow and district, joining in prayer at this historic site. The tradition, begun in 1975, of alternating the chair of the *Council of Churches* between Anglicans, Catholics and Free Churches, is expressive of the better inter-church understanding whose clearest realisation can be seen in the present '*Churches Together*' movement: its purpose might be said to be that of applying to all who follow Christ the mandate imposed on Catholics by the Second Vatican Council:

> We must get to know the outlook of our separated fellow Christians. To achieve this purpose, study is of necessity required, and this must be pursued in fidelity to the truth and with goodwill.[10]

St Mary of Furness today

Amidst these ecumenical developments, in 1979, St Mary's parish considered that it should proceed to re-order the church in line with the Council's liturgical specifications, and one of Fr Bickerstaffe's great contributions to the parish was to supervise this important work. The wooden altar, temporaly installed to comply with the new edict, was replaced by an impressive one in Italian marble weighing three tons, from the Carrara quarries which once supplied Michelangelo. It took five weeks to construct, at a cost of £1,500, and was made in three sections which took four days to fit and install in the newly elevated sanctuary.[11] The requirements of the renewed liturgy also meant that the physical barrier of the altar rails between priest and people had to go, though since it was felt that these were too beautiful to destroy, an inspired decision was made to reverse them, incorporating them into the kneelers for the front pews, where they remain. The gates of the altar rails, which had led into the sanctuary, on which were carved the *Ecce Homo* and *the Mater Dolorosa* were re-modelled to make two *prie-dieu* used for the bride and groom at weddings. To emphasise that Christ is present in both the Scriptures and the Eucharist, equal importance had to be given to the Table of the Word, and the Table of the Sacrament. To achieve this, the pulpit was removed and a new ambo, carved from Japanese oak, was placed convenient for the lay readers. The pews had all been stripped and re-varnished, a new central-heating system installed and the church decorated from top to bottom, when on the 15 August, the Feast of the Assumption of the Blessed Virgin Mary, the titular feast of the church, there was a grand reopening and evening Mass was concelebrated by the Bishop of Lancaster, the Rt Rev. B. C. Foley together with Bishop Hardman, a retired missionary.

The re-ordering of the church was not the only responsibility that Fr Bickerstaffe had to face. St Aloysius' school was expanding, and it was found necessary to amalgamate in 1979 with Our Lady's school. This new complex was now on two sites taking the title of St Bernard's, which recalled the Cistercian connection with area. As a school governor he faced increased responsibility as St Bernard's expanded.

Fr Bickerstaffe had both the cause of ecumenism and conciliar changes at heart, and made sure that St Mary's church was a worthy edifice for the new liturgy; he had been a most sociable priest, always enjoying company and one of the most generous of men. When he went on holiday to the United States in the first week of July 1985, his parishioners wished him God-speed and looked forward to his return. At evening Mass on Thursday 18 July the congregation were stunned to hear that Fr Bickerstaffe had died suddenly of a heart attack while on holiday. The personal message of the senior curate, Fr Murphy, to the parishioners in the Parish Bulletin of 28 July says it all:

> Dear Brothers and Sisters, you can imagine the cold shock I felt when I arrived in Lourdes and received the news of Fr Bickerstaffe's death. I know how shocked and saddened you all were by his death. After his eighteen years at St Mary's we shall miss him for a long time to come. I personally shall never forget his kindness to me. One of his favourite quotations – he always liked to let us know he knew his Latin! – was: *SI MONUMENTUM REQUIRIS, CIRCUMSPICE.* (If you wish to see his memorial look around you).[12] Each week as we enter the church which he so beautifully and tastefully renovated, we shall surely be reminded to pray for his soul.

The funeral had to be delayed for formal medical reports to be prepared in the United States before the body could be released for the Requiem celebrated on Thursday 25 July, 1985. The Rt Rev. John Brewer, Bishop of Lancaster concelebrated with many deanery and diocesan priests. Fr Howe, a priest friend with whom he had been on holiday, delivered the panegyric.

Canon Francis Cookson, ordained priest in 1953, who had spent the first few years of his priestly ministry as a curate at St Mary's, came from St Herbert's at Windermere in 1985 as the next parish priest. Before entering Ushaw College, the northern seminary at Durham in April 1947, he had been called-up to do his military service in the Royal Navy in January 1945.

Further implementation of, and instruction on Vatican II were revived by Canon Cookson, with particular attention to the preparation of a large number of extraordinary ministers of the Eucharist whose responsibility was initially to take Communion to the sick and house-bound and subsequently, when Communion under both kinds was introduced locally, also to administer the Chalice during Mass. 'Bidding Prayers', or The Prayers of the Faithful, which in medieval times had been part of the liturgy, were re-introduced, becoming mandatory, and Canon Cookson made sure that they were indeed the 'prayers of the faithful' and not the prayers of the priest, by insisting that members of the parish community compose them. Liturgy, adult education, laity involvement, colaborative ministry courses, the formation of a Parish Advisory Committee, and sacramental programmes, are only some of the many things Canon Cookson instigated. The spirit of Vatican II was his inspiration. He took to heart the Council document on Ecumenism, playing a full role in the ecumenical scene: when the *Churches Together in Barrow* decided to split the town into area working groups, as sub-divisions of the parent body, Canon Cookson became the first chairman of the Hindpool area group. On 18 July 1993, at a special celebratory Mass to mark the fortieth anniversary of his ordination, the parish gave thanks and this was followed by a lunch for all parishioners who wished to attend.

Catastrophe struck St Mary's on 9 February, 1988 in the shape of Hurricane K. A trail of havoc was left in its wake, not least on the spire and steeple of the church. Very fortunately, no one was injured, the only casualty being a parked car which was slightly damaged. The whole of Howard Street and Duke Street, the two streets adjacent to the church had to be closed to traffic; the church was unsafe to use; part of the steeple had crashed

FIGURE 25.
First public Mass
celebrated at Furness
Abbey since the
surrender, 13 June
1992. (*By courtesy of
the* North West
Evening Mail)

through the organ loft, damaging the organ, and eventually landed in the
church porch. The scene was reminiscent of that greeting the worshippers
on 4th May 1941, the morning after the Barrow Blitz. Once again, as during
the church re-ordering, St Mary's parishioners had to resort to the church
hall for Mass. The cost of the storm damage was £100,000, though fortunately this was covered by insurance. What the parish was not prepared
for was the report from the architect that the church would need complete
re-roofing, which was not covered by insurance. It was at this point that
it was found what the true extent of the war damage had been, unknown
all these years. The sandstone fabric of the church had been giving cause
for concern for some time, owing to the salt-laden prevailing winds and
industrial pollution, but the repairs to the steeple exposed even more
erosion damage through pollution than was at first thought. In particular,
it was found that stone-tracery of the rose window was almost worn through
in places, and would cost £18,000 to replace. The collapse of the steeple of
course brought down the cross surmounting it. A replacement was made
of fibre-glass, painted black with some gold paint incorporated into it, and
made by a local Walney yacht builder, Alan Newton. With the cross in
place, St Mary's began to look like a church once more.

This extra expense was, of course, not covered by the insurance, but St
Mary's parishioners were no strangers to the task of raising money and
fund-raising swung once more into action, with a vengeance. The ongoing
repair work and the expense it entailed has been a constant problem, but
by the generosity of the parishioners, and careful financial management of
Canon Cookson, gradually the debt to the diocese was cleared. At the time

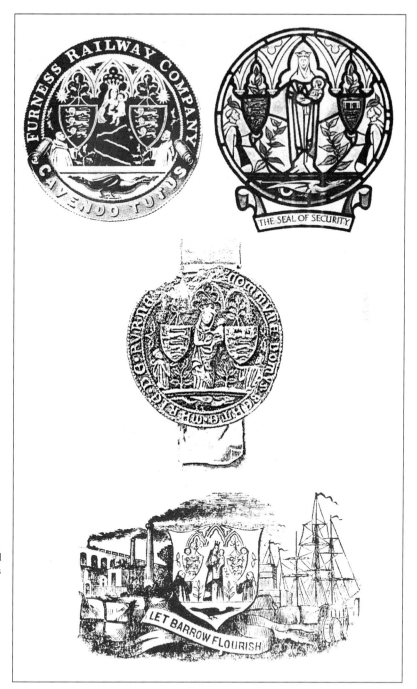

FIGURE 26.
The legacy of Furness Abbey. The abbey seal (centre) and its use as a logo by the Furness Building Society (top right), the Furness Railway Company (top left) and on the masthead of the *Barrow Herald* (bottom).

when the repair of the storm damage was carried out, some 'first-aid' work was done on the rose window, as the cost of replacement was considered too costly, but it eventually proved unsatisfactory and later a more permanent solution had to be found, causing even more expense. The interior of the church also had to be redecorated after all the building work was completed, and the church re-carpeted. When all this work was complete, and the parishioners once again returned to their church, a thanksgiving Mass was held at 7.00 p.m. on Wednesday 29 November 1989.

St Mary's has been fortunate in having many talented needlewomen, and in July 1990 an embroidery exhibition was held in the church to give the people of the town an opportunity to see, not only the work done by the parishioners, but exhibits by other local needlework artists. On show were various banners, quilts, ordination vestments, cross-stitch pictures, and embroidered kneelers from our sister church, St Mary's Anglican church, Walney. However, the highlight of the exhibition, was the opportunity to see some sixteenth and seventeenth century vestments kindly loaned by Mgr P. McKinney, rector of Oscott College, Birmingham.

For twelve years, Canon Francis Cookson steered the parish on an even keel. The parish has looked to him for fatherly support, and he has been noted for his kindness and desire never to hurt anyone's feelings. He has faced the heavy responsibilities of governorship of two schools and problems relating to an ageing school building only partially used for parish activities and showing the inevitable signs of age. Now he has earned his retirement and has been transferred to a smaller parish, St Bernard's at Knott End, Blackpool, Lancashire. The parish now, although feeling the loss of Canon Cookson, 'the big fella' as someone affectionately called him, has welcomed their new parish priest, Fr Stephen Cross, a younger man, who has to face the challenge of taking St Mary of Furness, Barrow, into the twenty-first century. He has a proud history to follow.

Barrow, throughout the twentieth century, has had its ups and downs; the years of both world wars produced a high level of employment, although between the wars there was great depression. Barrow led the way in both commercial and naval ships but as air travel has increased, so the demand for passenger liners has declined and the orders for these ships has dried up. Submarines had always played a high role in the naval programme and Vickers Shipbuilding and Engineering Limited (V.S.E.L.) concentrated on building these, so when the Ministry of Defence began to include nuclear submarines in its programme it was to V.S.E.L. that the Polaris order went, the first order being placed in May 1963, and when subsequently they got the Trident contract, in April 1986, Barrow became a boom town. However, the 'peace dividend' consequent on the end of the Cold War has had its price, and Barrow is now suffering the worst level of redundancies from V.S.E.L., the chief employer in the town, since the shipyard was built. As the number of redundancies rises, so the number of St Mary's parishioners who are employed goes down and it is to their credit that St Mary of Furness is still paying its way. In conjunction with the *Churches Together in Barrow*, ways are being explored to try to bring help and re-training to the unemployed, and to the school leavers who need alternatives to the traditional apprenticeships with V.S.E.L. which have now practically ceased. The town was successful in 1996, in winning an S.R.B. (single regeneration bid) from the Government, which it is hoped will bring more prosperity to the town. Some of this money, together with European funding is being chanelled into addressing the unemployment problem. We hope and pray that the town may come through this period of depression as it has done through similar times in the past.

Barrow has throughout most of its life been dependandant on ship building as the main souce of employment; and a great majority of the ships built, both during and since the first war have been for the Admiralty and latterly for the Ministry of Defence. This has caused difficult moral decisions having to be made; weighing up the needs of national defence and employment against the arguments for disarmament. During the 1920s and 1930s there was an active *League of Nations Union* in Barrow, which strove for total disarmament, the secretary of which, John Hemer, was a Catholic, the Anglican Bishop of Barrow, the Rt Rev. Herbert Sidney Pelham the president, and a member of the Society of Friends a committee member. (Another case of incipient ecumenism.) During the twenties, much soul-searching was suffered by this group and they experienced a certain amount of resistance in the town. Naval orders were considered to be essential for the economic stability of Barrow. Since the Trident programme has been bringing employment and prosperity to Barrow, the Campaign for Nuclear Disarmament, some of whose members have been Catholic, have been extremely active in demonstrations, especially on each occasion of the launch of a nuclear submarine. It has always been difficult being a pacifist in Barrow. Fortunately, the future holds out hope; orders have been received and executed for surface merchant vessels, and its hoped that these will increase.

This history began with the Abbey of St Mary of Furness and it is only fitting that the circle should be completed and finish where it began. A Franciscan friar, Fr Bruno Rowswell, O.F.M. (Cap), walking round the ruins of Furness Abbey in 1991, was so overcome with emotion that he exclaimed to his companions: 'We should have a celebration here, a celebration of Mass'. This idea was taken up, Bishop Brewer was approached and he was only too pleased to agree. On the 13 June 1992 this celebration was held; the Rt Rev. John Brewer, Bishop of Lancaster, concelebrated Mass with the priests of Barrow. A very large congregation filled the ancient nave, people coming from all over the deanery and beyond. Whereas in 1927, when the 800th centenary was celebrated, it poured with rain, this time the sun shone and it was a glorious day. The altar was erected in the area which had been the original sanctuary of the abbey, and for the first time for 450 years the Mass, the centre of Catholic worship was once again celebrated publicly within the abbey church. Beck said, when recording the surrender of the abbey: '. . . the lamp of St Mary's altar was extinguished forever.'[13] On this memorable day in 1992 that lamp was re-lit. Let us hope that it will not be the last time.

Notes

1. Michael Walsh, *An Illustrated History of the Popes Saint Peter to John Paul II* (London: Marshall Cavendish Editions, 1980), p. 224; Eamon Duffy, *Saints and Sinners – A History of the Popes* (New Haven and London: Yale University Press in association with S4C, 1997), pp. 271–79; Peter Hebblethwaite, *The Runaway Church* (London: Collins, 1975).

2. Norman P. Tanner (ed.), with G. Alberigo *et al.*, *Decrees of the Ecumenical Councils* (2 vols, London: Sheed & Ward, Washington D.C., Georgetown University Press, 1990), vol. II, pp. 820–43.

3. Ibid., vol. II, pp. 908–20.

4. Verbal information received from Ian Linden of the Catholic Institute for International Relations (C.I.I.R.) the successors of 'The Sword of the Spirit'.

5. Verbal information received from the late Mr H. McGinley, quondam Honorary Treasurer of the Barrow Council of Churches.

6. Extracts from Minute Books of *the Barrow and District Council of Churches*, now *The Churches Together in Barrow* (Lodged with the current secretary, not in the public domain).

7. Ibid.

8. Ibid.

9. Extracts from Minute Books of *the Dalton and District Council of Churches*, now the *Dalton Christian Council* (Lodged with the current secretary, not in the public domain).

10. Tanner, *Decrees*, p. 910 .

11. *North Western Evening Mail*, 14 August 1979.

12. Inscription on the floor of St Paul's Cathedral, London. Referring to Sir Christopher Wren.

13. Beck, *Annales*, p. 349. See chapter 2.

APPENDIX 1

Extract from the annual letters of the English Province of the Society of Jesus for 1688

In December last the house in which Fr Clement Smith lived was beset by a mob of nearly 300 men out of whose hands he managed to escape through the Providence of God; for he was about to leave the house by a passage which would have afforded easy entrance to the mob, when one of the rioters, for some unknown cause, shouted to those rushing on, that there was no way there, on hearing which they desisted from their intention of breaking in at that place. Time was thus allowed for Fr Smith to escape by another way. He passed that night in a little hut; at daybreak, however, he betook himself to the woods, where he remained fasting the whole of that day, suffering much from intense frost and the snow which covered the ground. Night coming on, the people of the neighbourhood refused through fear, or from the reviving hatred towards Catholics, to allow him to shelter in their barns or hovels. Compelled therefore to seek some other place of refuge for the night he crept into a deserted hut and at early dawn next morning betook himself again to the woods, his pursuers still following close on his track. A short time after this he had an extremely narrow escape while travelling with a man who was acting as his guide. They met a party of pursuivants, who strictly examined the guide, yet seemed not to notice the Father, for they did not address a word to him, but allowed them to pass on their way unmolested. Frequently in the darkness of the night he was obliged to cross on foot through fords and passes rendered exceedingly dangerous by reason of the ebb tide, so that travellers on horseback were unable to make the passage by daylight without considerable risk of life. [Obviously the quicksands of Morecambe Bay.] For three months he was compelled to lie so closely hidden that he was unable even to pace about his room, nor durst he for a whole year together use either fire or candle, lest he be betrayed by the light. Indeed for the space of two years he was unable to leave the house where he was charitably harboured.

APPENDIX 2

Dom. John Dionysius Huddleston, O.S.B.

John Dionysius Huddleston was born 15 April 1608, at Farington Hall, in Leyland Hundred, Lancashire, son of Joseph Huddleston of that place, his mother of Kikbarrow, Westmorland. The family also owned land at Hutton John, Cumberland. It is highly probable that being born into one of the Catholic gentry families of the northern counties he was already acquainted with John Preston whose family also fell into that category, before he was sent to Douai college to be educated. Although his name does not appear in the Douai Diaries, it is understood that he was ordained there as a secular priest. After ordination it is not surprising that he returned to the north part of Lancashire taking up a position as chaplain to the Prestons at the Manor. What is surprising is that he, a priest, should have enlisted in the army (on the evidence of Pepys), under John Preston, who raised a civil war royalist regiment with his own money. One can only assume that, as a priest, and thereby forbidden under canon law to bear arms, that he served as a military chaplain. As he was in (by now) Sir John's regiment it is likely that he was with Sir John when he suffered his fatal wound at Furness, and it was to his friend that Sir John looked when considering the future of his heir, the young Sir John who was only five years old. The boy was staying with his grandmother, Mrs. Morgan in Warwickshire; the abbey estates having been confiscated for royalist 'malignancy' by Parliament, during this period, so he committed his young son into the care of John Huddleston. In 1651, after the Royalist defeat at the battle of Worcester, as is well known, Huddleston was instrumental in saving the life of King Charles II. At some undated point in his busy life, he was professed as a Bededictine, and at the Restoration became a chaplain to the queen-dow-ager, Henrietta Maria, widow of Charles I, at Somerset House. After her death he was appointed chaplain to Charles II's queen, Catherine of Bra-ganza with a generous salary of one hundred pounds and a pension of a similar amount. While there, he reconciled Charles II to the Church on his deathbed.

APPENDIX 3

'Barrow as it was'. Extract from the *Barrow Herald* – Issue 23, October 1871

... There are three churches (C. of E.) St George's (1861) Vicar Rev. T. S. Barrett; St James (1868) Rev. R. P. Manclarke; St Paul's (1871) still not completed but in use, Rev. T. Goss; Presbyterian Lecture Hall (Church of Scotland) Rev. Ferguson; Methodists, Hindpool Road Chapel ... but the largest body of Christians are those connected with the Latin Church, and as Macaulay was unable to conceive the possibility of that community ever ceasing to be what it has been, we, as journalists are in duty bound to record the position which it has attained in Barrow. By the ecclesiastical organisation of the Roman Catholic Church, Barrow-in-Furness forms part of the diocese of Liverpool and are therefore under the jurisdiction of the Rt Rev. Dr Goss. This 'mission' as regards Catholicity was first established by the appointment of the Rev. J. Bilsborrow as first resident priest in March 1865. Until that time the Catholics of this neighbourhood were compelled to resort to Ulverston. On the arrival of their priest however, they rallied round him, their numbers largely increased and their prospects rapidly brightened. The Duke of Devonshire, through we believe, the agency of Mr Ramsden, granted them a valuable site of land in Duke Street for the erection of a church, schools and priest's house. Meanwhile, Mr Walmsley generously allowed the use of a room over his shop in Newland, and there for more than two years, like early Christians in the Catacombs, one hundred Catholics had to assemble for mass on a Sunday in a room which, when crowded to suffocation could scarcely contain one hundred souls. Sunday after Sunday those who could not gain admission were seen kneeling among the oil-casks and turpentine barrels in Mr Walmsley's shop or on the pavement in the yard at the back of his house. Sometimes even, a crowd might have been seen kneeling in the open street. The inconvenience from which both the pastor and people suffered during this trying noviciate in all probability stimulated their exertions and inflamed their zeal and charity. Fr Bilsborrow often appealed to the working man – of which class his congregation almost exclusively consisted – to give each a day's wage to the Building Fund of the new church, and his expectations were, each time, more than realised by the hearty response of his people. So successfully did the work progress that a sum of money was collected sufficient to justify them in beginning to arrange for the building of the church ... The number of Catholics in Barrow we are informed, are not less than 2,500.

Bibliography

Primary sources

Manuscript sources

Archives of the Society of Jesus, Mount Street, London: Rixton-Wigan Papers of the College of St Aloysius.

British Museum, Cotton MS., Cleopatra, EIV, fol. 134

British Museum, Lansdown MS, 75,fo. 44

British Museum, Lansdown MS, 56,fo. 174

Public Record Office: (DL 26) Duchy of Lancaster, Conveyancing of deeds; (DL 29) Ministers' accounts; (DL 41) Letters and Papers relative to the Dissolution of Conishead, Prior's 1st Offer, Prior's 2nd Offer.

Public Record Office, SP1/75, fol. 63; SP12 *Dom. Eliz.* 33.

Lancaster Diocesan Archives, Bishop's House, Lancaster, Documents of St Mary's,Barrow.

Cumbria Record Office Barrow, ZS 1170 (Letter to Bishop of Chester)

Lancashire Record Office, RCHY 3/7/11, 25, 26, 56; RCLJ, ACC. 5919/1

Printed primary sources

Archives of the Society of Jesus, Mount Street, London: Foley, H. (ed.), *Records of The English Province of the Society of Jesus*, 7 vols (1977–83)

Bardsley, C. L. and Ayre, L. R. (eds), *The Registers of Ulverston Parish Church* (Ulverston, Lancs: James Atkinson, 1886)

Barrow Guardian (4 June 1927; 23 July 1927)

Barrow Herald and Advertiser (25 June 1864; 24 June 1865; 14 July 1866; 23 Aug. 1867; 7 Sept. 1867; 13 June 1868; 13 May 1871; 23 Oct. 1871; 4 Nov. 1871; 10 Feb. 1872; 9 March 1872; 17 Aug. 1872; 14 Sept. 1872; 10 Oct. 1872; 13 May 1873; 9 May 1874; 2 Feb. 1876; 23 Feb. 1876; 25 Nov. 1876; 7 July 1877; 22 Oct. 1878; 23 Nov. 1878; 16 Sept. 1879; 4 Jan. 1881; 8 Feb. 1881; 9 April 1881; 13 May 1882; 25 Nov. 1882; 30 Oct. 1883; 13 Nov. 1883; 24 May 1884; 2 Jan. 1886; 7 Feb. 1887; 20 Oct. 1888; 21 Sept. 1889; 14 Oct. 1899)

Barrow News (21 Sept. 1889)

Bodius, H., *Unio dissidentium* (Cologne, 1531)

Caffrey, E., *Catholicity in Barrow*, Barrow Reference Library, Lc200F/CAF (n.d.)

Calendar of State Papers, Spanish 1485–1558 20 vols (1862–1954), vol. 11.

Caley, J. and Hunter, J. (eds), *Valor Ecclesiasticus*, 6 vols (1810–34)

Camden Miscellanea, Camden Society vol. 9 (1895)

Casson, T. E. (ed.), 'The Diary of Edward Jackson, Vicar of Colton, for the year 1775', *Transactions of the Cumberland and Westmorland Antiquarian and Archaeological Society*, new series, vol. 40. (1940), pp. 1–45.

Catholic Family Annual and Almanac for the Dioceses of Liverpool and Shrewsbury (1899–1902; 1912)

Catholic Record Society, *Lancashire Registers III, Northern Part*, vol. 20 (1916)

Catholic Record Society, *Lancashire Registers, The Fylde II*, vol. 16 (1914)

Catholic Record Society, *Miscellanea*, vol. 4 (1907)

Catholic Record Society, *Recusant Rolls 2, 1593–4*, vol. 57 (1965)

Catholic Record Society, *Recusant Rolls 3–4, 1595–6*, vol. 61 (1970)

Catholic Record Society, *Unpublished Documents relating to the English Martyrs 1584–1603*, vol. 5 (1908)

Cumbria Record Office, Barrow, BPR/21 I37/1 (Open Letter – Parliamentary Leaflet)

Elsas, M. (ed.), 'Deeds of the Parish of Crosthwaite (1571–1636)', *Transactions of the Cumberland and Westmorland Antiquarian and Archaeological Society*, new series, vol. 45 (1945), pp. 39–48

Elton, G. R. (ed.), *The Tudor Constitution: Documents and Commentary* (Cambridge: Cambridge University Press, 1962)

'Father Allan's First and Second Reply to Rev. Mr Bardsley' in *Historical Papers* (1903), privately bound collection of pamphlets in author's possession, to be deposited at the Talbot Library, Preston

Historical Manuscripts Commission: Le Fleming Manuscripts (London: HMSO, 1890)

Jackson, C. (ed.), 'The Life of Master Shaw', in *Yorkshire Diaries and Autobiographies in the Seventeenth and Eighteenth Centuries*, Surtees Society, vol. 65, Durham (1877), pp. 121–61

Kelly, P. V., *The Banner of St Mary of Furness*, Barrow Reference Library (leaflet), Lc200FE/Ban, Mary (n.d.)

Kendall, W. B. and Gaythorpe, H. (eds), 'The Village of Barrow – Owners and Occupiers, 1843, with Supplementary Notes', *Annual Reports, Proceedings etc. of the Barrow Field Naturalist Club, and Literary and Scientific Association*, vol. 17 (1909), pp. 181–91.

Lancaster Diocesan Directory (1970)

Letters, Foreign and Domestic of the reign of Henry VIII, 23 vols (1862–1932), vol. 6, 11(1); 12(1); 12(2); 13(1).

North Western Daily Mail (24 Feb. 1925; 9 July 1927; 16 July 1927; 28 May 1931; 11 Jan. 1932)

North Western Evening Mail (3 May 1945; 28 June 1965)

Pickering, D., *Statutes at Large*, 1225–1806 (46 vols, London: Cambridge University Press, 1762–1807), vols 10, 13, 32, 37.

Raine, J. (ed.), *Wills and Inventories from the Registry of the Archdeaconry of Richmond*, Surtees Society, vol. 26 (Durham, 1853)

Soulbey's Ulverston Advertiser and General Intelligencer (8 Oct. 1863)

Strype, J., *Ecclesiastical Memorials relating chiefly to Religion and the Reformation of it, and the Emergence of the Church of England under King Henry VIII, King Edward VI, and Queen Mary I* (1721) Reprint 19 vols (Oxford: Clarendon Press, 1822)

Tanner, N. P. (ed.), *The Decrees of the Ecumenical Councils* (2 vols, London: Sheed and Ward, 1990)

The Register of the Guild of Corpus Christi in the City of York, Surtees Society, vol. 57, Durham (1872)

Valor Ecclesiasticus, 6 vols (1810–34), vol. 5.

West, T., *Antiquities of Furness, or an Account of the Royal Abbey in the Vale of Nightshade, near Dalton in Furness, belonging to The Right Honourable Lord George Cavendish* (London: 1774, 2nd edn, William Close, London: Walker, 1805)

Wordsworth, W., *Selected Poems of William Wordsworth* (London, New York, Toronto: Oxford University Press, 1950)

Worrall, E. S. (ed.), *Returns of Papists 1767*, 2 vols, Occasional Papers Series, Catholic Record Society (1980–9)

Secondary sources

Allison, A. F. and Rogers, D. M., *Biographical Studies 1534–1829, Recusant History*, vol. 1. (1951–2)

Anstruther, G., *The Seminary Priests, 1558–1659* (4 vols, Great Wakering: Mayhew–McCrimmon 1968–77), vol. 2.

Barnes, F., *Barrow and District* (Barrow-in-Furness: The Barrow Printing Co., 1968)

Baskerville, G., *English Monks and the Suppression of the Monasteries* (paperback edn, London: Jonathon Cape, 1937)

Beck, T. A., *Annales Furnesienses: History and Atiquities of the Abbey of Furness* (London: Paynes & Foss, 1844).

Bellenger, D. A, *The French Exiled Clergy in the British Isles after 1789: An Historical Introduction and Working List* (Bath: Downside Abbey, 1986)

Billington, R. N. and Brownhill, J., *St Peter's Lancaster* (London and Edinburgh: Sands & Co., 1910)

Blackwood, B. G., *The Lancashire Gentry and the Great Rebellion*, Chetham Society, 3rd series, vol. 25 (1978)

Bossy, J., *Christianity in the West: 1400–1800* (Oxford: Oxford University Press, 1985)

Bossy, J., *The English Catholic Community 1570–1850* (London: Darton, Longman & Todd, 1975)

Bouch, C. M. L. and Jones, G. P., *A Short Economic and Social History of the Lake Counties* (Manchester: Manchester University Press, 1961)

Boumphrey, R. S., Hudleston, Roy, C., and Hughes, J., *An Armorial for Westmorland and Lonsdale, CW* Extra Series, vol. 21, Gateshead (1975)

Broxap, E., *The Great Civil War in Lancashire (1642–1651)* (Manchester: Manchester University Press, 2nd edn, 1973)

Bulmer, J., *History and Directory of Furness and Cartmel* (Preston: Snape. n.d.)

Burgess, J., *Christians in Cumbria* (Kendal: Titus Wilson, 1982)

Cameron, E., *The European Reformation* (Oxford: Clarendon, 1991)

Centenary Celebrations: The Church of St Mary of Furness, Barrow-in-Furness, 1865–1965 (Desktop publication), Barrow Reference Library, LC200 FE/Chu, Mary (n.d.)

Chambers, R. (ed.), *A Biographical Dictionary of Eminent Scotsmen* (Glasgow, Edinburgh and London: Blackie & Sons, 1854)

Duffy, E., *The Stripping of the Altars: Traditional Religion in England 1400–1580* (Cambridge: Cambridge University Press, 1993)

Duffy, E., *Saints and Sinners* (New Haven and London: Yale University Press in association with S4C, 1997)

Elton, G. R., *Policy and Police: The Enforcement of the Reformation in the Age of Thomas Cromwell* (London: Cambridge University Press, 1966)

Emminghaus, J. H., *The Eucharist* (Collegeville, MN: Liturgical Press, 1988)

Erickson, C., *Bloody Mary: The Life of Mary Tudor* (London: Robson Books, 1978)

Foley. B. C., *Some People of the Penal Times* (Preston: Snape, 1991)

Foley, B. C., *Some Other People of the Penal Times* (Preston: Snape, 1991)

Fraser, A., *The Gunpowder Plot: Terror and Faith in 1605* (London: Weidenfeld & Nicolson, 1996)

Gillow, J., *Bibliographical Dictionary of English Catholics* (5 vols, 1885–1902)

Gilley, S., and Sheils, W. J., *A History of Religion in Britain. Practice and Belief from Pre-Roman Times to the Present*, Oxford and Cambridge Mass.: Blackwell, 1994)

Graeff, H., *Mary: A History of Doctrine and Devotion* (2 vols, London and New York: Sheed and Ward, 1963)

Haigh, C., *Reformation and Resistance in Tudor Lancashire* (Cambridge: Cambridge University Press, 1975)

Haigh, C., *The English Reformations* (Oxford: Oxford University Press, 1993)

Haigh, C., *The Last Days of the Lancashire Monasteries and The Pilgrimage of Grace*, Chetham Society, vol. 17, Manchester (1969)

Hamilton, B., *Religion in the Medieval West* (London: Edward Arnold, 1986)

Harrison, S., *The Pilgrimage of Grace in the Lake Counties, 1536–7* (London: Royal Historical Society, 1981)

Haydon, C., *Anti-Catholicism in Eighteenth-century England, c. 1714–80. A political and social study* (Manchester and New York: Manchester University Press, 1993)

Hebblethwaite, P., *The Runaway Church* (London: Collins, 1975)

Hickey, J., *Urban Catholics, in England and Wales from 1829 to the Present Day* (London, Dublin and Melbourne: Geffrey Chapman, 1967)

Hilton, J. A., *Catholic Lancashire: From Reformation to Renewal 1559–1991* (Chichester: Phillimore, 1994).

Holmes, J. D., *More Roman Than Rome: English Catholicism in the Nineteenth Century* (London: Burns and Oates, 1978)

Holmes, J. D. and Bickers, B. W., *A Short History of the Catholic Church* (Tunbridge Wells: Burns & Oates, 1983).

Holt, T. G., *William Strickland and the Suppressed Jesuits* (Southampton: Hobbs, 1988)

Joy, D., *A Regional History of the Railways of Great Britain: Railways of the Lake Counties* (Melksham, Wilts: David St John Thomas, 1990)

Kenyon, J., *The Popish Plot* (London: Heinemann, 1972)

Kenyon, J., *Stuart England*, 2nd edn (London: Penguin Books, 1985)

Knowles, D., *The Religious Orders in England* (3 vols, Cambridge: Cambridge University Press, 1961)

Loades, D., *The Reign of Mary Tudor: Politics, Government and Religion in England 1553–58*, 2nd edn (London and New York: Longman, 1991)

McCoog, T. M., *English and Welsh Jesuits 1555–1650*, Catholic Record Society monograph, vol. 74 (1994)

McGrath, P., *Papists and Puritans under Elizabeth I* (London: Blandford Press, 1967)

Meyer, A. O., *England and the Catholic Church under Queen Elizabeth* (London: 1916, 2nd edn, London: Routledge and Kegan Paul, 1967)

Midmer, R., *English Medieval Monasteries, 1066–1540 (Summary of)* (London: Heinemann, 1979).

Miller, J., *Popery and Politics in England, 1660–1688* (London: Cambridge University Press, 1973)

Mullett, M., *The Counter-Reformation and the Catholic Reformation in Early Modern Europe* (London: Methuen, 1984)

Mullett, M., *James II and English Politics* (London: Routledge, 1994)

Muir, T., *Stonyhurst College 1593–1993* (London: James & James (1992)

Norman, E., *The English Catholic Church in the Nineteenth Century* (Oxford: Clarendon Press, 1984)

Page, W., *Victoria History of the Counties of England, Lancashire, vol. 8* (1914), reprint (1966)

Plumb, B., *Found Worthy* (Warrington: B. Plumb, 1986)

Rubin, M., *Corpus Christi: The Eucharist in Late Medieval Culture* (Cambridge: Cambridge University Press, 1994)

Scarisbrick, J. J., *Henry VIII* (Cambridge: University Press, 1968)

Stephens, L. and Lee, S. (eds), *Dictionary of National Biography*, 63 vols (1895–1900)

Tierny, M.A. (ed.), *Dodd's Church History of England from the commencement of the sixteenth century to the Reformation in 1688* (5 vols, London: Charles Dolman, 1839–43)

Walsh, M., *An Illustrated History of The Popes Saint Peter to John Paul II* (London: Marshall Cavendish Editions, 1980)

Ward, T. G. and Warren, L., *The Manor Mission of Low Furness* (Bolton: The Catholic Printing Company of Farnworth, 1979)

Widdup, H. L., *Christianity in Cumbria* (Kendal: Titus Wilson, 1981)

Woodward. G. W. O., *The Dissolution of the Monasteries* (London: Blandford Press, 1966)

Wrightson, K., *English Society 1580–1680* (London: Unwin Hyman, 1982)

Articles

Blackwood, B. G., 'Plebeian Catholics in the 1640s and 1650s', *Recusant History*, vol. 18 (10) (1986), pp. 42–50.

Carleton, K. W. T., 'English Catholic Bishops in the Early Elizabethan Era', *Recusant History*, vol. 23, no. 1 (1996), pp. 1–14.

Curwen, J. F., 'St Anthony's Chapel, Cartmel Fell' *Transations of the Cumberland and Westmorland Antiquarian and Archaeological Society*, new series, vol. 12 (1912), pp. 285–296.

Duffy, E., 'William Cardinal Allan 1532–1594', *The Venerablile*, vol. 30, no. 5 (1995), pp. 7–28

Fowler, J. T., 'On the Painted Glass at St Anthony's Chapel, Cartmel Fell' in *Transactions of the Cumberland and Westmorland Antiquarian and Archaeological Society*, new series, vol. 12 (1912), pp. 297–311

Hilton, J. A., 'The Cumbrian Catholics', *Northern History*, vol. 16 (1980), pp. 40–58

Holt, T. G., 'Father West, F.S.A.' *Transactions of the Cumberland and Westmorland Antiquarian and Archaeological Society*, new series, vol. 79 (1979), pp. 131–138.

Morris, K. L., 'Rescuing The Scarlet Woman: The promotion of Catholicism in English Literature, 1829–1850', *Recusant History*, vol. 22, no. 1 (1994), pp. 75–86.

Mullett, M., 'A Catholic Looks at Quakerism', *Quaker Studies*, vol. 2, no. 1 (Sunderland: University of Sunderland, 1997), pp. 57–64.

Newman, P. R., 'Roman Catholic Royalists: Papist Commanders under Charles I and Charles II, 1642–1680', *Recusant History*, vol. 15, no. 6 (1981), pp. 396–404.

Unpublished theses

Borwick, D., *An English Provincial Society, North Lancashire 1770–1820* (unpublished Ph.D. thesis, University of Lancaster, 1994)

Pearson, S. G., *Apostolicae Curae (1896): Its reception in Britain 1896–1897), and the theological issues arising from it.* (unpublished STB thesis, Katholieke Universiteit, Leuven, 1989)